LINDISFARNE LITURGIES
FOR CHRISTIAN FESTIVALS

LINDISFARNE LITURGIES
FOR CHRISTIAN FESTIVALS

RAY SIMPSON

Augsburg Books
MINNEAPOLIS

The Liturgies that appear in this book are drawn from
'Liturgies from Lindisfarne' by Ray Simpson.

Acknowledgements

We are grateful to the following for permission to include their prayers in this publication:

Page 63: From *The Book of Common Order of the Church of Scotland* (St Andrew Press, 2007). © Church of Scotland Panel on Worship.

Page 156: John L. Bell. Copyright © WGRG, c/o Iona Community, Glasgow G2 3DH, Scotland. Reproduced by permission. www.wgrg.co.uk

LINDISFARNE LITURGIES FOR CHRISTIAN FESTIVALS

© Copyright 2015 Ray Simpson.

Original edition published in English under the title LINDISFARNE LITURGIES FOR CHRISTIAN FESTIVALS by Kevin Mayhew Ltd, Buxhall, England.

This edition published in 2020 by Fortress Press. All rights reserved. Except for brief quotations in critical articles or reviews, no part of this book may be reproduced in any manner without prior written permission from the publisher. Email copyright@augsburgfortress.org or write to Permissions, Fortress Press, PO Box 1209, Minneapolis, MN 55440-1209.

Unless stated otherwise, Scripture quotations are taken from *The New Revised Standard Version of the Bible*, copyright © 1989 Division of Christian Education of the National Council of the Churches of Christ in the USA. Used by permission. All rights reserved.

Cover image: © Unsplash 2020: Castle Silhouette during sunrise by Louis Watson
Cover design: Emily Drake

Print ISBN: 978-1-5064-6004-8

Contents

About the author	6
Introduction	7
Advent	9
The Nativity or Christmas	29
Epiphany or Theophany of Christ	45
Lent	59
Holy Week	75
Easter	95
Ascension	109
Pentecost	119
Trinity	131
Remembrance of Saints	143
Declarations	153

About the author

Ray Simpson is a Celtic new monastic for tomorrow's world, a lecturer, consultant, liturgist, and author of some 30 books. He is the founding guardian of the international Community of Aidan and Hilda (www.aidanandhilda.org) and the pioneer of its e-studies programmes. He is an ordained member of the Christian church and lives on the Holy Island of Lindisfarne. His website is www.raysimpson.org

Introduction

With joy you will draw water from sources that sustain.
Isaiah 12:3

These prayers provide worship for individuals, new monastic groups and churches that reconnect the post 9/11 world with the seasons and the soil, the saints' and the streets, the struggles, senses and silence, as well as the Spirit and the Scriptures.

These inclusive patterns of worship are provided by the international Community of Aidan and Hilda and draw from early and contemporary Celtic devotion, Anglican, Orthodox, Reformed and Roman Catholic sources.

Although these liturgies are international they are used daily in the chapel of the Community's Retreat House on The Holy Island of Lindisfarne (The Open Gate) and certain prayers have been inspired by the island or used in its churches.

Advent

In Advent we contemplate the coming among us of God in Christ, and the fact that all people have to give account to God who comes as the light that exposes darkness. We recall witnesses to Christ before his birth and people's aspirations today which Christ can fulfil.

In order for something divine to be cradled and born in us, we seek, during Advent, to be as Mary was before the birth of Christ – believing, waiting, praying, inviting the Holy Spirit to work within us.

In the West, Advent begins on the fourth Sunday before Christmas. In Celtic tradition, as in today's Orthodox churches, it begins forty days before Christmas.

Advent Candle-Lightings

An Advent wreath contains a large white candle in its centre. This represents Christ, Light of the World, and is lit on Christmas Day. Four (or in the Celtic tradition, six) purple candles surround it. One is lit in the first week of Advent, two in the second week, and so on.

The Candle-lightings may precede any of the Advent Prayer Liturgies or stand alone.

The sixth week before Christmas

The candle of the coming of the kingdom of God
One candle is lit.

I light a candle to remind us of the darkness before Jesus came,
and we remember the greater light that will dawn when he returns.
I light this to remind us of God's Word spoken through prophets long ago,
and we remember that God still speaks through faithful messengers today.
I light this to remind us of the divine kingdom which is among us now,
and we remember to prepare ourselves for the greater kingdom which is still to come.

The fifth week before Christmas

The candle of light in our darkness
Two candles are lit.

We light a candle for every person who has pointed to a world of good that surely is to come, and has shone like a light in the dark.

**Eternal Light, shine into our hearts.
Eternal Goodness, deliver us from evil.
Eternal Power, be our support.
Eternal Wisdom, scatter the darkness of ignorance from our path.**

The fourth week before Christmas

The candle of people's longings
One/three candles are lit.

We light the first/third candle of Advent.

The candle of longing,
the candle of solidarity with the yearnings of the people
and with the hopes of our forebears in faith.

ADVENT

Where people long for an end to injustice,
shine into their hearts.
Where people long for conflict to cease,
shine into their hearts.
Where people long to right inhuman working conditions,
shine into their hearts.
Where people long to restore the scarred places of earth,
shine into their hearts.
Where people long for dignity in human relationships,
shine into their hearts.

The third week before Christmas

The candle of prophets' urgings
Two/four candles are lit.

We light the second/fourth candle of Advent.

This is the candle of prophets calling for justice,
struggling for right to replace wrong,
for dignity to replace oppression,
the candle of prophets calling for desolate places to be renewed,
pointing to light emerging from the darkness.

The second week before Christmas

The candle of preparers of God's coming
Three/five candles are lit.

We light the third/fifth candle of Advent.

The candle of the preparer,
clearing away human resistance to God,
humbling the monuments to human pride,
giving voice to those who have no voice,
a sign of those who point the way to Christ,
who overturn false ways,
who live by the values of God.

The week before Christmas

The candle of those who bring Christ to birth

Four/six candles are lit.

We light the fourth/sixth candle of Advent.

This is the candle of Mary who bears the Divine Glory, the candle of purity, the candle of all midwives of faith who bring the Divine to birth.

Morning Prayer

Opening In the wasteland may the Glory shine.
In the land of the lost may the King make his home.

or

Let us wake to Christ's summons,
urgent in our midst:
**let us wake to the truth that
his power alone will last:**
the worlds that now scorn him
will vanish like a dream.
**When God takes back his own,
all good will be one stream.**

Singing or music

Psalm Psalm 50; 75; 76; 94; 139:1-6, or 139:19-24

Forgiveness Week 1

All-knowing God,
poets and parents-in-God picture and pattern your ways;
forgive us for following idols and illusions.

Pause

Week 2

All-seeing God,
prophets shine like candles in the night;
forgive us for staying in the dark.

Pause

Week 3
All-holy God,
forerunners like John clear obstacles from
your path;
forgive us for blocking your way.

Pause

Week 4
All-giving God,
the Virgin Mary offered her all as the bearer of
your life;
forgive us for holding ourselves back.

Pause

Lord of creation, King of the last judgement,
immortal, holy and mighty,
you sit with the book of life and death open
before you.
All mortals pass before you, one by one, like sheep.
In your book of life all our deeds are written.
You see our hearts, you know our every thought.

There may be silence or Kyrie Eleison and a declaration of forgiveness such as the following:

The All-merciful God forgive you for past sins
and free you to do good.

Old Testament reading Let us attend, the Word of God comes to us.
**Illumine our hearts, O Lord, implant in us a desire for your truth;
may all that is false within us flee.**

Isaiah 40:1-11 or the reading of the day

ADVENT

Pause, singing or the following:

A Song of the Wilderness
Parched land shall laugh and bloom and sing of God's glory.
The lame shall leap like young deer.
Waters shall gush out and streams shall flow in the deserts.
The people God restores will have everlasting joy.
Joy to the world.
Glory to the God who comes.

Echoes verses from Isaiah 35

New Testament reading

Let us attend; Christ, the living Word, comes to us.

Matthew 24:36-44 or the reading of the day

This is the Word of Christ.
Praise to the coming King.

I wait for the Lord, my soul waits and in God's Word I put my hope.
Saviour of the world, come to us.

My soul waits for the Lord, more than those who watch for the morning.
Saviour of the world, come to us.

O people, hope in the Lord!
For with the Lord there is steadfast love and full redemption.
Saviour of the world, come to us.

In our darkness there is no darkness with you, Lord.
With you, the deepest dark is as clear as the day.
Saviour of the world, come to us.

*Or 'We bless you' (The Song of Zechariah) –
see Declarations, page 154.*

There may be singing, activity or teaching.

Intercessions *Any of the following prayers may be said.*

Calm us to wait for the gift of Christ.
Cleanse us to prepare the way for Christ.
Teach us to contemplate the wonder of Christ.
Anoint us to bear the life of Christ.

Alternate lines of the response may be read by two groups, e.g. male and female, those sitting on the left and right.

Help us to prepare a way for you
1 **by our thoughtfulness towards others,**
2 **by our care in little deeds,**
1 **by our upholding of the oppressed,**
2 **by our thoughtful use of things,**
1 **by our care of crops and kitchens,**
2 **by our upholding of creation.**

The earth is becoming a wasteland.
Breath of the Most High, come and renew it.
Humanity is becoming a battleground.
Child of Peace, come and unite it.
Society is becoming a playground.
Key of Destiny, open doors to our true path.
The world is becoming a no-man's land.
God-with-us, come and make your home here.

There may be free prayer on the above themes.

From December 17

Come, Wisdom, Breath of the Most High,
Bough of creation, permeating all that lives
with the birth pangs of suffering love, come
and teach us your ways.
Maranatha, come, redeeming Lord.

Come, head of the family of Israel. You
revealed yourself to Moses in the fire of the
burning bush and gave him laws to guide his
people; come and dispel our confusion.
Maranatha, come, redeeming Lord.

Come, descendant of Jesse, King David's
father, you are a sign to the nations. The
world's rulers will give way to you, the
world's people will summon your aid; come
and free us from oppression.
Maranatha, come, redeeming Lord.

Come, heir of King David, the Majesty of
every people, the key to their destiny.
You open doors that none can shut; you close
doors that none can open.
Come and lead us to our destiny.
Maranatha, come, redeeming Lord.

Come, Morning Star, bright Sun of Justice,
bring light to all who are in the darkness of
ignorance or self-will. Come and bring us
eternal light.
Maranatha, come, redeeming Lord.

Come, Cornerstone of the new world to be
built. You formed us of the one earth, you
make opposing peoples one. Come and save
us from destruction.
Maranatha, come, redeeming Lord.

Come, Emmanuel, God with us. Wonderful Counsellor, you understand all people, you are the Hope of all nations, come to live among us.
Maranatha, come, redeeming Lord.

There may be silence, the Lord's Prayer or singing.

Closing **The King of life appear to us;**
the Son of life shed light on us;
the Spirit of life flow into us;
the Holy Three come near to us.

ADVENT

Midday Prayer

Opening Christ, Light of the world,
meet us in our place of darkness.
Christ, Light of the world,
meet us in our place of longing.
Christ, Light of the world,
meet us in our place of working.

Advent candle-lighting or light one candle saying:

I light this candle, as a sign of the King who comes to rule.

Jesus, our health, rule in our bodies.
Come, Lord Jesus, come.
Jesus, our worth, rule in our work.
Come, Lord Jesus, come.
Jesus, our love, rule in our households.
Come, Lord Jesus, come.
Jesus, our life, rule in our living and dying.
Come, Lord Jesus, come.

Old Testament reading God says, 'Establish justice and do what is right, for soon my salvation will come and my deliverance will be revealed.
Isaiah 56:1, 2

Among the hungry,
among the homeless,
among the friendless,
come to make things new.

Among the powerful,
among the spoilt,
among the crooked,
come to make things new.

In halls of fame,
in corridors of power,
in forgotten places,
come to make things new.

With piercing eyes,
with tender touch,
with cleansing love,
come to make things new.

New Testament reading Just as Jesus has left you for heaven, so he will come again.
Acts 1:11

**Restore to us, Lord, what has been eaten away.
Bring into being what is yet to be.**

There may be silence, singing, free prayer or the following prayer:

All-wise God, sourcing and permeating creation,
source and permeate us.

Civilising God, who revealed laws that brought good order out of cruel anarchy,
civilise us.

Redeeming God, who through your regents rescued your people from hell and destruction,
rescue us.

God of Destiny, the Key that unlocked the greatness of great David's kingdom,
unlock the greatness of our lives and our land.

ADVENT

Morning Star, who dispersed the gloom of
your oppressed people,
**cheer our spirits and put sin and neglect
to flight.**

Emmanuel, God-with-us, who came to live in
a lost and lonely world,
make your home with us today.

Closing You call your people,
you gather those who have strayed,
you, the One who is coming.
Gather us to you in the middle of the day
and keep us faithful until your appearing.
**May we be a hand to the weak,
an anchor in the storm
and a light in the dark.**

Evening Prayer

On special occasions this may be preceded by a candle-lit vigil of silence, or drum beats that build up a sense of anticipation. An Advent wreath may be placed on a table.

Opening Heaven, shed your dew
clouds, rain down salvation.
Earth, bring forth the Saviour.

There may be singing.

Psalm The following extract or Psalm 50:1-6; 52; 75; 85; 89:46-52; 94:1-15; or 102:1-16

O God, I long for you from early morning; my whole being desires you. Like a dry, worn-out and waterless land, my soul is thirsty for you.

Let me see you in the place of prayer; let me see how glorious you are. Your constant love is better than life itself, and so I will praise you.

I will give thanks as long as I live. I will raise my hands to you in prayer. My soul will feast and be satisfied, and I will sing glad songs of praise to you.

Psalm 63

Praise the One who comes.
Praise the One who came.
Praise the One who calls us now to greet the highest Name.

Old Testament reading   Isaiah 44:1-8 or the reading for the day

Where times are dark,
where wrong parades as right,
where faith grows dim,
we pray for light.

**Christ, Light of the world,
meet us in our place of darkness,
journey with us
and bring us to your new dawning.**

New Testament reading   1 Thessalonians 5:1-11 or the reading for the day

The following may be said or sung to the tune Abbotsleigh.

**You are holy, you are whole,
let earth give praise from pole to pole.
You are coming, coming here
to bring your hard-pressed people cheer.
Bringing to them human birth,
born of heaven, born of earth.
Bringing to them bread and wine,
giving hope of life divine.**

Meditation, teaching, activity or singing.

Intercessions   Desire of every nation, we bring to you those who are empty and who long to find meaning.
Come to them, Lord Jesus.

Desire of every nation, we bring to you those who are overlooked and who long to know their worth.
Come to them, Lord Jesus.

Desire of every nation, we bring to you those
who are exploring, but who do not know what
they search for.
Come to them, Lord Jesus.

Lord, you keep us waiting for signs of hope;
you keep us looking for ways in which
you come.
The pain of the world, the anguish of the people
cry out to you.
Come, Lord Jesus, come.

We pray for blighted areas;
make them bloom . . . *(examples may be given).*
In your mercy,
come, Lord Jesus, come.

We pray for those who are shut out from your
Presence;
bring them in . . . *(examples may be given).*
In your mercy,
come, Lord Jesus, come.

We pray for our homes;
make them places of peace and light . . .
(examples may be given).
In your mercy,
come, Lord Jesus, come.

We pray for those who govern;
may peace and justice mark their rule . . .
(examples may be given).
In your mercy,
come, Lord Jesus, come.

We pray for our places of learning;
make them sources of truth and wholeness . . .
(examples may be given).
In your mercy,
come, Lord Jesus, come.

We pray for those who are dying;
may perpetual light shine upon them . . .
(examples may be given).
In your mercy,
come, Lord Jesus, come.

There may be free prayer, silence or singing.

Closing God be with us on our journey towards Christmas.
Help us to go deeper into what is real,
until we are brought to the wonder of your birth
and know your incarnate love afresh.

Night Prayer

In the southern hemisphere use the alternative to the opening sentence and 'We wait in the darkness'.

Opening In darkest night we pray, may the Light of lights come to us.
We wait for the Lord more than those who watch for the morning.

Silence, confession, or meditative singing.

Bible reading Psalm 4; 17:1-8; 139:7-12; or Isaiah 45:2-8; 55:6-11; or Psalm 119:9-18 (fourth week)

We wait in the darkness, expectantly, longingly.
Come, O God Most High.

In the darkness we can see the splendour of the universe – blankets of stars, the solitary glowings of the planets.
Come, O God Most High.

In the darkness of the womb mortals are nurtured and the Christ-child was made ready for the journey into light.
Come, O God Most High.

In the darkness the wise three found the star that led them to you.
Come, O God Most High.

In the darkness of dreams you spoke to Joseph and the wise ones and you still speak to us.
Come, O God Most High.

In the darkness of despair and distress we watch for a sign of hope from the Light of lights.
Come, O God Most High.

Alternate lines of the following may be read by two groups, e.g. male and female, those sitting on left and right.

1 **O God of life, darken not to us your light.**
2 **O God of life, close not to us your joy.**
1 **O God of life, soften to us your anger.**
2 **O God of life, crown to us your goodness.**

A candle is lit.

Christ is the light that comes into the world.
A light that no darkness will quench.

There may be singing.

Bible reading Jesus said, 'I am the light of the world. Whoever follows me will not walk in darkness, but will have the light of life'.

John 8:12

Son of the prophets, on our longings,
let your light shine.
Son of Mary, on our littleness,
let your light shine.
Son of Eternity, on our lying down,
let your light shine.
Let us ask that the Light shine also on those in darkness and on those we love.
Let us name them now in silence or aloud . . .

Closing For the darkness of night enfolding the day's labour,
we bless you, dear God.
For the sweetness of sleep restoring the tired frame,
we bless you, dear God.

Call forth this night bearers of your presence,
that we may we rest in the undying flame of your love
and wake to the light of your dawning.

Alternatives for the southern hemisphere:

Opening

At this time of Advent, fire our imaginations with the sweep of your salvation. Catch us up in the cause of your kingdom that is near to breaking through.

God, your Advent feet

God, your Advent feet come silently along our noisy streets;
the noise, our ears, the silence contain the Christ we fail to greet.

God, your Advent feet come silently along our noisy streets;
the noise, our ears, the silence contain the Christ we fear to meet.

God, your Advent feet come silently along our noisy streets;
the noise, our ears, the silence contain the Christ we long to greet.

The Nativity or Christmas

In the Celtic Christian tradition Christmas is known as the Nativity. In common with the rest of the universal Church in the West, 25 December was chosen as the official date when Jesus' birth would be celebrated. The actual date of Jesus' birth is not known. Orthodox churches in Celtic lands who use the new, revised Julian Calendar now also celebrate the Nativity on 25 December; other Orthodox churches celebrate it on 6 January. Christmas worship begins on Christmas Eve, 24 December, and continues for twelve days, from 25 December until Epiphany (6 January in the Western Church).

Prayers at a Crib Service

May we journey with you, Jesus,
Mary and Joseph,
to your birthplace at Bethlehem,
firm in the faith,
loyal to the truth,
obedient to your Father's will
along the path that leads to life.

God bless this crib:
as we look at the face of Jesus, may we see the glory of eternity shining now among us; the tenderness of God here beside us now.

God bless this crib:
as we look at the face of Jesus, may we see the One who patterns goodness and heals the world.

God bless this crib:
as we look into the face of Jesus, may we see the splendour of the Divine Father, and the fruit of a human mother, a brother to us all.

God bless this crib:
as we look into the face of Jesus, may we see the Prince of Peace, the joy of angels, the meaning of a human life.

A single candle may be lit in front of the crib, or the five candles of an Advent wreath may be lit as follows.

Jesus, born of Mary *(light first candle)*,
light up our darkness.

Jesus, proclaimed by angels *(light second candle)*,
light up our darkness.

Jesus, worshipped by shepherds *(light third candle)*,
light up our darkness.

Jesus, adored by wise people *(light fourth candle)*,
light up our darkness.

Jesus, God who is with us now *(light the fifth central candle)*,
light up our darkness.

Now is born Christ the King of greatness:
now is the time of the great Nativity.
**Glow to him wood and tree;
glow to him mount and sea;
glow to him land and plain;
come to him, people, and let him reign.**

Morning Prayer

Opening You, whose cupped hand contains the sea,
are born in a cave.
**Your glory fills the heavens
and the manger is filled with your splendour.**

Great is the amazement of this earth of ours,
that the Lord of all has come down to it,
has become a human being.
The Ancient has become a child.
The Master has become like his servants.
The King's Son as someone despised.
Glory to God who has come to live among us.

St Ephrem

There may be singing.

Christ, born of the loveliest Mary,
you are with us at this time (on this day) of joy.
**The eternal Son of God
is with us evermore.**

Psalm Psalm 97, 98, 46, 115, or 105:1-11

Forgiveness *If a Confession/Forgiveness is desired the following may be used.*

Jesus, God's Gift of Love,
forgive the hurts I have caused.

Jesus, God's goodness,
**forgive me for filling my life with things
that have no lasting good.**

Jesus, truly God, truly human,
forgive me for not being my true self.

There may be singing.

Old Testament reading Isaiah 62:1-5 or the reading of the day

**Glory and honour to you, our God,
for revealing your love in human flesh.
Glory and honour to you, our God,
for filling Mary with the life Divine.
Glory and honour to you, our God,
for sharing our life on earth.**

New Testament reading Luke 2:1-14 or the reading of the day

Thanksgiving The soles of his feet have reached the earth;
the soles of the Son of Glory.
All the world gives homage to him;
the sun on the housetops shines for him.
The voice of the winds with the song of the streets;
announce to us that Christ is born.
God the Lord has opened a door;
the Door of Hope, the Door of Joy.
Golden Sun of earth and sky;
all hail! Let there be joy!

There may be singing, meditation teaching, or creative activity.

Intercessions Babe of heaven, you had to travel far from your home;
strengthen us on our pilgrimage of trust on earth.

Defenceless Love, your birth shows us the wonder of being human;
help us to live fully human lives for you.

King of glory, you come among the poor with
justice and peace;
help us to serve others as you serve us.

*There may be free prayer after each of the following
petitions, followed by the response.*

May each and every mother and child be
cherished as Mary cherished you.
Lord, in your mercy . . .
Hear our prayer.

May each person who seeks a room to live in
not have the door shut in their face.
Lord, in your mercy . . .
Hear our prayer.

May those who are out in the cold find a
sanctuary as warm as yours.
Lord, in your mercy . . .
Hear our prayer.

May those who work by night respond to your
presence, as the shepherds did.
Lord, in your mercy . . .
Hear our prayer.

There may be free prayer and singing.

Closing May the cares of the past grow dim,
may the skies and our hearts grow clear
**until the Son of God comes to meet us
striding on this earth.**

Midday Prayer

Opening *A candle is lit.*

Marvellous exchange!
The Creator takes our flesh!
Truly human, yet owing us nothing.
Lord, what you give us is your being.
Your Being is your Goodness.
Your Goodness is your Love.

Meister Eckhardt

New Testament reading Mark 3:35 or the following

Glory to God in the highest
and on earth peace, and good will among all.

Luke 2:14

Glory to God in the highest.

Psalm Psalm 96:1-9

Jesus, you are
the Holy Babe,
the Shepherd of your flock,
the Healing Person,
Pattern of goodness,
Brother of the poor,
Champion of justice,
Emmanuel, God-with-us.

Jesus, you are
the Glory of eternity shining now among us,
Prince of Peace,
Wonderful Counsellor,
Joy of angels,
Friend of all.

There may be silence or music.

Intercessions Your birth made possible the holy family;
make families whole and holy today.

May the Holy Child not be lost amid tinsel
and trifles.
**May the Holy Child emerge among the
peoples of our time.**

Jesus, born in a stable,
make here your home.
Jesus, born of a peasant girl,
make here your home.
Jesus, searched for by wise seekers,
make here your home.
Jesus, reared at a carpenter's bench,
make here your home.
Jesus, with us now,
make here your home.

There may be silence or singing.

Be with us, Lord, in the middle of the day,
keep us in the spirit of Bethlehem.
**Keep us
in the faith of Mary
in the trust of Joseph
and in the simplicity of the shepherds.**

Blest are the pure in heart;
they shall see God.

Blest are the meek;
they shall inherit the earth.
Matthew 5:3, 5

*There may be free prayer, the Lord's Prayer
and singing.*

Closing The blessing of God be with us.
The Son of God beside us.
The angels of God around us.
The joy of God within us.

On Christmas Day
These prayers may be said before or after the main meal instead of Midday Prayer.

The earth gave you a cave,
the skies gave you a star,
the angels gave you a song,
at this feast we will give you our love.

The love that Mary gave her Son,
may we give to the world.

The love that you give us through your Son,
may we give back to you.

Evening Prayer

Opening When peaceful silence lay over all, and night had run half of her swift course, your all-powerful Word, O Lord, leaped down from heaven, from the royal throne.
**Glory to the Most High God
who has come to live among us.**

There may be singing.

Psalm Psalm 8 or the psalm of the day

Son of the star, Son of the dawn,
Son of the heavens, Son of the earth,
Son of Mary, Son of God,
is dwelling now among us.
Alleluia!

Old Testament reading Isaiah 52:1-5 or the reading of the day

When the ride is bumpy

When the ride is bumpy and the world passes us by,
you are God with us.

When we are edged aside and doors are shut in our face,
you are God with us.

When others are out to get us and our home is not secure,
you are God with us.

When our lives are but a flicker in the encroaching dark,
you are God with us.

New Testament reading Matthew 1:18-25 or the reading of the day

There may be silence, teaching, activity or singing.

Intercessions We thank you for the holy family which began with Mary, Joseph and Jesus. We thank you that you wish every person on earth to become part of that family. Deepen our holiness, that we may be embraced into the heart of your family today.

Jesus, in you we see God's face smiling upon us –
strong and kind.
In you, may we find
gentleness as the answer to violence;
tenderness as the answer to ill-will;
truth as the answer to lies;
hope as the answer to despair.

There may be other prayers, free prayer or singing.

Closing May the long-reaching gladness of Christmas stretch far down the days before you, surrounding you with the goodness of Christ, child of love, teacher of truth, man of sorrow, conqueror of death, dwelling with you for ever.

Night Prayer

Opening Night stars gleam o'er mountains high,
God almighty journeys nigh.
The soles of his feet have touched the earth,
the soles of the Son of glory.

There may be this or another song.

Glory to you, our God this night,
for all that's dawning on our sight.
Glory to you, dear Mary's Son
who scatters far our dark and gloom.

O Babe of Heaven, defenceless Love,
you left for us your home above.
You come to take us in your hand.
Let all give thanks throughout the land.

Tune – Tallis' Canon

Bible reading Psalm 110:1-4; 126:1-3; or Isaiah 11:1-5

Marvellous exchange! The Creator takes flesh!
Truly human, God is now with us.
Alleluia!
Tonight we may rest in peace.
Alleluia!
You who were born of the Virgin Mary
be born in us tonight.
God with us, come, gently enfold us
as we rest in trustful calm.

In silence or aloud blessings are recalled.

New Testament reading Luke 1:41-53 or Colossians 1:15-19a

Child of glory, Child of Mary,
born in a stable, King of all.
Your greatness holds the universe.

Hold also
those who are sleeping rough,
those who feel shut out of society,
those who are cold and hungry,
and these we name before you now . . .

May the light of Bethlehem shine on these
dear ones tonight.

There may be singing.

Closing Love's furnace was hidden in a little room,
**homemaker God, come to our homes
this night.**
As it was in the stillness of the morning,
so may it be in the silence of the night.
As it was in the hidden vitality of the womb,
so may it be in the hidden life of our sleep.
Prince of peace,
your peace be on us at the ending of this day.
In the fellowship of Mary and Joseph, in the
joy of the shepherds, the angels and the Lord,
we shall lie down in peace.

Additional Prayers for the days following Christmas Day

26 December St Stephen's Day

Today is the first day after the birth of Christ.

Today shepherds leave their flocks and make time to wonder at the birth of God's Son.

Today we leave our routines and live in the wonder of this sacred birth.

Yesterday our King left heaven, put on the robe of flesh, and brought earth the gift of love.

Today a soldier leaves his body of earth and goes to heaven out of love for the King.

Today is the day of Stephen, the first of the martyrs for Christ.

Today is the first day of Christmas, when we shall give our all.

27 December St John

Today is the second day after the birth of Christ.

Your beloved disciple taught us that you became a human being that we might become children of God.
Lord, make us your family.

Your beloved disciple took your mother to himself.
Lord, make us your family.

28 December The slaughter of innocent infants in Bethlehem
Today is the third day after the birth of Christ.

By being born you made every birth sacred, yet tyrants resist this truth. King Herod, seeking to kill all rivals, ordered Bethlehem's infant boys to be killed.

Today we remember that you remain God with us.
In you truth is stronger than falsehood, light is stronger than darkness, love is stronger than hatred, and life is stronger than death.

The first Sunday after 28 December or a nearby weekday The Holy Family
Today is the ___ th day of Christmas.

Today we remember the little family of Mary, Joseph and Jesus which in love embraced the large family of animals, angels and neighbours.

Their forebears sprang from first human stock and were God-guided folk. This family carried in its heart that vast family of all who love Jesus as their brother.

30 December Today is the fifth day after the birth of Christ.

May we be as Mary to those in whom Christ is being born.

May we be as Joseph, giving faithful service, to guard what God is doing.

As Brigid was a nursemaid of Christ, so shall we be today.

31 December in Western calendars — New Year's Eve

Today is the sixth day after the birth of Christ, God who took flesh from the blood of generations.

As we leave behind one year and prepare to live another,
give us forgiveness towards all who have hurt us,
discernment to know what you have brought about,
the will to step onto the springboard that another year offers.

1 January — New Year's Day, the Naming of Christ, Basil of Caesarea

Today is the seventh day after the birth of Christ, when Jesus was given his name in the temple and we usher in a new year.

Eternal God, as your servant Basil proclaimed how by your incarnation you gathered into one things earthly and heavenly, gather all that we are and do this coming year into the divine glory, that it may shine in us now and through the ages.

2 January — Seraphim of Sarov

Today is the eighth day after the birth of Christ.

Out of the silence of eternity your Word brought life to the world.

Out of the silence of the forest your servant Seraphim spoke words that brought life to a people, and your divine warmth was incarnate in the frozen snows of Russia.

Out of the stillness of our devotion may your Word bring life to us.

Epiphany or Theophany of Christ

This season celebrates the showing forth of Christ's presence to the world. It is known as Epiphany in the Western Church and Theophany in the Eastern Church.

It is an extension of Christmas and begins twelve days after Christmas – 6 January in the Western Church.

Its themes are:

The wise men taking knowledge of the infant Christ back to their countries (week one).

The baptism (immersion) of Christ into the human life-stream and the world into Christ (week two).

The transformation of everyday life and creation, symbolised by the changing of water into wine (week three).

The unifying of the whole created world with Christ (week four for Christian unity).

The light spreading across the world underlies it all.

Morning Prayer

Opening Arise, shine for God's rays of glory spread across the earth.
**The Sun of suns is rising,
rulers and peoples shall be drawn to the light.**

There may be singing and candle-lighting.

One I welcome the light that dances in the rising sun.
Two I welcome the light that dawns in the Son of God.
Three I welcome the light that gleams through the growing earth.
Four I welcome the light that you kindle in our souls.

There may be singing.

The first week of Epiphany – the light spreads

Psalm
Psalm 72:1-19 or the psalm of the day

Incense may be used.

As gold is purified in fire,
purify us that we may be royal priests to you.
We offer ourselves to you as gold.

As the rising incense speaks of your Presence,
may our hearts always rise to you in adoration.
We offer ourselves to you as incense.

As myrrh spreads the fragrance of perfume,
may our beautiful deeds be fragrant to you.
We offer ourselves to you as myrrh.

Old Testament reading
Isaiah 60:1-6 or the reading of the day

The second week of Epiphany – The People's Representative is immersed in the Stream of Life

Psalm
Psalm 29 or the psalm of the day

The Immortal who bowed the heavens bows his head before a mortal.
Glory!
The Uncreated enters the stream of created life.
Glory!

God becomes one with us, and we are made
one with God.
Glory!
Our lost innocence is restored and the world is
charged with the grandeur of God.
Glory!
Father love cascades over the Son; the Spirit
pours upon him;
God in Trinity is revealed.
Glory! Glory, ever and everywhere!

Water may be sprinkled.

Old Testament reading
Genesis 1:1-5 or the reading of the day

The third week of Epiphany – God transforms the ordinary into the extra-ordinary

Psalm
Psalm 36:5-10

You transform water into sparkling wine.
You transform our drabness into vibrant joy.
Glory to you, Father, glory to you.
Glory to you, Saviour, glory to you.
Glory to you, Spirit, glory to you.

Old Testament reading
Isaiah 62:1-5 or the reading of the day

The fourth week of Epiphany – Christ unifies the whole created world

Psalm
Psalm 133, 122 or the psalm of the day

In Christ there is no longer Jew and foreigner,
there is no longer slave or free,
there is no longer male or female,
all are one in Jesus Christ.

Old Testament reading
Ezekiel 37:15-28 or the reading of the day

Declaration From the womb of Mary light streams forth.
From the womb of earth light streams forth.
From the womb of the church light streams forth.

**Lord, flood the world with light,
shine into the drab places
and fill those who wait for you with your glory.**

New Testament reading Matthew 2:1-12 (week 1); Matthew 3:13-17 (week 2); John 2:1-11 (week 3); Colossians 1:15-23 (week 4); or the reading of the day

There may be teaching or singing.

Intercessions May the star of justice shine in our world, especially in places where injustice holds sway.
**Pour into the empty cups of the world,
the beauty and blessings of Christ ...**
(Examples may be given.)

May your Presence
reveal your mother heart of compassion
and draw together your children.
**Pour into the empty cups of the world,
your abounding love and compassion.**

There may be singing.

Closing May God, who laboured in love to create all life
continue creating new vision and life in us.

EPIPHANY OR THEOPHANY OF CHRIST

Midday Prayer

The Christ candle is lit.

Opening The Light of Christ
open our eyes to your presence shining here among us.

New Testament reading 2 Corinthians 4:5, 6

Jesus,
truly God, truly human.
Your greatness holds the universe,
your goodness beckons us,
your wisdom searches us,
your generosity enriches us,
your strength spurs us,
your mercy frees us.

The face of Christ now shines upon us,
may our hearts become bright with the light of God.

Draw us to your light,
may your glory spread across the earth and may people see your wonder.

or

1 Corinthians 10:1-4

As Christ enters the stream of created life,
we are immersed in the stream of divine life.
As Christ comes up out of the water,
the world is charged with the glory of God.

O Saviour, who takes away the sins of the world,
immerse us in the waters of your Presence;
**the waters that cleanse,
the waters that heal,
the waters that renew your life in us.**

Jesus, you are the Living Water who sustained our forebears.
Immerse in your Presence our lives, our lands, our world.

Silence or singing.

You are a holy nation, a royal priesthood, a people who belong to God, that you may declare the praises of the One who called you out of darkness into God's wonderful light.

1 Peter 2:9

Psalm Open up the gates
that the king of glory may come in.
Who is the king of glory?
The Lord Almighty, he is the king of glory.

From Psalm 24

You who are hidebound and defensive,
open up the gates; let in the King of glory.

You who harbour hatred and plan acts of violence,
open up the gates; let in the King of glory.

You who pursue selfish goals and thoughtless ways,
open up the gates; let in the King of glory.

You who . . .
open up the gates; let in the King of glory.

Christ, who makes all things new,
transform the frailty of our nature with the riches of your grace
and in the renewal of our lives
make known your heavenly glory.

Where there was fear
may there be trust.
Where there was greed
may there be faith.
Where there was darkness
may there be light.
Where there was strife
may there be peace.

We pray that this may be so in these people and places: *Anyone may name people or places.*

Silence, singing or the Lord's Prayer.

Closing May the glory and grace of God shine through us to the world.
Mary's Son beside us,
the Spirit deep within us.

Evening Prayer

Opening A star leads the wise three to the infant King of all.
Alleluia.

In the waters of baptism Jesus is revealed as Christ.
Alleluia.

In the water made wine Christ revealed a new creation.
Alleluia.

Let us worship the Lord whose Glory streams towards us.

A Gloria or other song or silence.

Psalm Psalm 113 or the psalm of the day

Let us say together:

Holy, holy, holy is our God Emmanuel, present with us now.

Music, or all may sing 'Faithful vigil ended' or another song.

Old Testament reading Isaiah 60:1-3 or the reading of the day

Let us affirm our faith:

**Christ was revealed in human form,
shown to be right by the Spirit,
worshipped by angels,
proclaimed among the nations,
believed in throughout the world,
taken up into heaven.**

A very early Creed – 1 Timothy 3:18

EPIPHANY OR THEOPHANY OF CHRIST

New Testament reading John 1:29-34 or the reading of the day

There may be singing or teaching.

Proclamation Christ, Splendour of the Father's glory,
sustaining the worlds by your Word of power,
renew your Presence in our lives.

Christ, begotten of the Father before time,
born at Bethlehem in time,
make us a sign of simplicity and joy.

Christ, our bright Morning Star,
when this world's darkness is past,
bring us into your eternal light.

or

Sinless Saviour,
you enter the stream of life and become one
with all creation,
you move through the waters,
and transform them with your glory.
**Glory to God, Source of all being,
Eternal Word and Holy Spirit.**

Intercessions *Silent, free or prepared intercessions may follow any of the headings below.*

May your light, O Christ, stream into the five continents;
Africa, America, Asia, Australasia, Europe . . .

May your light stream into seekers, people of all faiths and of none . . .

May your light stream into dark places of neglect, crime and conflict . . .

May your light stream into centres of
commerce, industry and government . . .

May your light stream into us, our homes and
communities . . .

From the rising of the sun to its going down,
God's name will be praised.

There may be singing.

Closing The Lord bless you, keep you
and be gracious to you.
The Lord's face shine upon you
and give you peace.

Night Prayer

Opening The earth has been made holy by your
holy birth.
The stars of heaven have proclaimed your glory.
Light now spreads across the earth.
And shines through us this night.

There may be music or singing.

Psalm Psalm 8 or 19:1-4

Glory to God.
Glory to God, creating.
Glory to God, redeeming.
Glory to God, lighting up the world.

In the coming of the wise three
you were revealed as king.
In your entering into the baptismal waters
you were revealed as Christ.
In your changing of water into wine
you revealed a new creation.
Transform our poverty into riches.
Transform our darkness into light.

We give thanks for signs of your Presence in the world . . . *Signs of Christ's presence are recalled in silence or aloud.*

As Jesus' parents dedicated him in the temple,
his glory was revealed to Simeon the old.

New Testament reading My eyes have seen your salvation,
a light for all peoples and glory for this people.

Luke 2:30-32

All sing or say 'Faithful vigil ended'.

*Let us pray for the light to shine on people and
places we now name in silence or aloud.*

I saw a new heaven and a new earth and the
holy city coming out of heaven like a bride.
A voice proclaimed:
now God will live with his people.
The city needs no sun or moon to light it
for its light is the glory of God
and in that light the peoples of the earth shall
find their way.
Verses from Revelation 21

Closing No more shall we languish in darkness or dread
for you shall be our everlasting light.
Bring us to that place where there is no
more sun.
**May we be
drawn by the light of God,
warmed by the fire of God,
bathed in the glory of God,
this night and for ever.**

EPIPHANY OR THEOPHANY OF CHRIST

A Candle-Lighting to Celebrate the Coming of Light

For use at any time, especially on 1 February (St Brigid) or 2 February (the infant Christ dedicated in the temple and revealed as Light of the World forty days after his birth).

1. One candle is already lit – Jesus – Light of the World.
2. In our darkness we light a candle of hope.
3. In our ignorance we light a candle of truth.
4. In our pain we light a candle of love.
5. In our wonder we light a candle of praise.

May all our lights together become one flame that warms the world with Christ.

This day also invites us to take a last look back to the joys of Christmas, and a first look towards the coming times of Lent and the Cross.

Prayer Northern Hemisphere

As the season of darkness recedes,
may the incoming light be to us the true Light
in whose presence no unworthy thought,
no deed of shame,
may stubbornly remain.

Southern Hemisphere

May the light within
sustain us in the time ahead,
and be kindled in a thousand hearts.

Lent

Introduction

This introduction may be said on Ash Wednesday, forty days before Easter, and on occasions thereafter.

In these forty days you lead us into a desert of reflection in which we withdraw from getting and spending and desiring, and, through fasting from the frenzied feeding of false desires, meditation on your Word, and acts of service you open our eyes to your presence in the world, free us to share your generous love and be again your pilgrim people.

We need time, space, simplicity in our lives – enough bareness to discern the outline of who we are. Lent is a time for clarity, as when the bare boughs of winter show us the shape of the tree in austere beauty. Let us clear away the clutter of our lives, in order to see the underlying pattern. Let us follow in the steps of our Saviour that by sharing his pain we may also come to celebrate the joy of resurrection.

Penitence and Ashes *If appropriate a sign of penitence, the sign of the cross, is made with ashes on the foreheads of those who wish this.*

You form us from the dust of the universe: may these ashes be a sign of our penitence, a symbol of our mortality, and a reminder that it is by your grace alone that we receive eternal life.

As each is signed:
Remember that you are dust and to dust you shall return. Repent and turn with all your heart to Christ.

Morning Prayer

Opening Let us return to God who is all forgiveness;
we will wait for the Lord more than those who watch for the dawn.

We seek to tread in the steps of Christ;
in the steps of Christ our Champion and King.

He has shown us the way when strong, when weak;
he is our Guide in everything.

Psalm Psalm 1; 25; 51:1-17; 78:1-8; 130; 131; or 139:1-18, 23, 24

Forgiveness We have fallen short of what you desire, O God: wipe clean our sins and save us.
Save us, O God.
You who saved Noah from the waves of the Flood,
save us, O God.
You who saved your people from an oppressor's hand,
save us, O God.
You who saved Jonah from the deepest abyss,
save us, O God.

or

Good God, you have created humankind to be immortal and an image of your own eternity; yet often we forget the glory of our heritage and wander from the path which leads to goodness. Look with mercy upon our frailties and forgive our shortcomings, that we may be filled with light, and reflect the strength of your love.

There may be a Declaration of forgiveness, music of lament or the singing of words such as 'Lord, have mercy'.

Old Testament reading Exodus 34:1-10; Leviticus 19:1-18; Deuteronomy 26:1-15; Amos 5:6-15; Hosea 8:11-14, 10:1, 2 or the reading of the day

Either

Strip from us what is not of you

Christ, who was born in an outbuilding;
you were with us in our birth.

Christ, who was thirty years at the carpenter's bench;
you are with us in our work.

You were driven to the sands by the searching Spirit;
strip from us what is not of you.

You were alone, without comfort or food;
help us to rely on you alone.

Though tested by the Evil One you clung to no falsehood;
break in us the hold of power and pride.

You followed to the end the way of the cross;
strengthen us to remain true to you to the end.

or

With Abraham . . . we wait *(see Declarations, page 155).*

or

The Cross, we shall take it *(see Declarations, page 156).*

Silence or singing

New Testament reading Luke 7:40-50; 12:1-12; 12:13-21; 12:22-34; 12:35-40; 12:41-48; 12:49-end; 15:11-31 or the reading of the day

By your self-giving in death
O Holy Fire,
O Holy Grace.

By your birth,
bring us life.

By your overcoming of troubled spirits,
make us strong.

By your integrity,
make us true.

By your fortitude in trials,
keep us firm.

By your self-giving in death,
make us generous.

By your mission to call unquiet spirits to rest in you,
raise us to eternal life.

There may be teaching, activity, singing or silence.

Intercessions *One of the following prayers may be used followed by silent reflection, free or led intercessions.*

God of all seasons,
in your pattern of things
there is a time for keeping
and a time for losing,
a time for building up
and a time for pulling down.
In this holy season of Lent
as we journey with our Lord to the Cross,
help us to discern in our lives
what we must lay down
and what we must take up,
what we must end
and what we must begin.

The Book of Common Order of the Church of Scotland

O God,
take from us cynicism, domination and idle chatter.
Give us wholeheartedness, patience and love.
Help us to see where we are wrong
and not to judge others.
For you are The Greatest through all the ages.

Echoes a prayer of St Ephrem the Syrian

Too long have I worried about so many things
and yet, my Lord, so few are needed.
May I live more simply – like the bread.
May I see more clearly – like the water.
May I be more selfless – like the Christ.

From Russia

I give you worship with my whole life.
I give you reverence with my whole understanding.

**I give you love with my whole heart.
I give you my all, O God of all gods.**

*There may be singing, the Lord's Prayer, free
prayer or a time of silent waiting.*

Closing   Great God,
as fish live in water
may we live in you.
As birds fly in air
may we move in you.
As trees stand in earth
may we stand in you.

or

May the God of strength be with us,
holding us in strong-fingered hands.
**May we be a sacrament of strength
to those whose hands we hold.
May the blessing of strength be on us all.**

Midday Prayer

Opening We draw aside in the middle of the day
to purge our desires and seek your face,
O Christ.

Psalm Psalm 119:1-8; 119:9-16; 119:17-24; 119:25-32;
119:33-40; 119:41-48; or 119:129-138

O God, create in us a clean heart,
**restore in us a true spirit,
cast us not away from your presence.
Renew in us the joy of salvation,
endow us with a generous spirit.
Then we will teach your paths to those who
have lost their way
and they will return to you.**

Silence or music

Let us pluck out by the roots Adam's sinful
greed in Eden that proved deadly to the world.
**Let us touch the Tree of the Cross
that pours out immortality on the world
like a new river from Paradise.
Through which all things will be made alive.**

or

Christ, you are the refined molten metal of our
human forge.
**Purge our desires,
strengthen our resolve,
sharpen our minds,
shape our wills.**

In our time of need and in the middle of the day
keep us thankful, true and faithful.

There may be singing.

New Testament reading Jesus said:
Blest are those who hunger and thirst for justice, for they will be filled.
Matthew 5:6

or

Blest are the merciful for they will be shown mercy.
Matthew 5:7

or

Blest are those who are persecuted for the cause of right, for theirs is the kingdom of heaven.
Matthew 5:10

Silence and free prayer.

Intercessions *Intercessions may be offered on the following themes, followed by saying or chanting of the Trisagion.*

**Holy God, Holy Mighty,
Holy Immortal, have mercy on us.**

We pray for mercy on ourselves . . .

Holy God . . .

We pray for mercy on the world . . .

Holy God . . .

We pray for mercy on these we name . . .

Holy God . . .

There may be singing or music.

Closing Let us bless the Lord.
**Working and praying
may we walk in the way of the Cross
each hour of this day.**

Evening Prayer

Opening Holy God, you call us to throw off whatever clouds your will.
We will struggle with Christ against wrong.
We will share with Christ his trials.
We will embrace with him the suffering of the world.

Psalm Psalm 25; 26; 27; 32; 34; or 52

There may be singing.

Forgiveness Father Creator, we have raped and spoiled your world,
God, forgive us.

Jesus Saviour, we have ignored your teachings and warnings,
God, forgive us.

Spirit Sustainer, we have tried to live without you,
God, forgive us.

For every sin we have ever thought or done,
God, forgive us.

For every thing we have sought outside your love,
God, forgive us.

For every wasted moment,
God, forgive us.

For every ill intent towards another,
God, forgive us.

For every failure of love towards your creation,
God, forgive us.

There may be silence, music of lament, sharing or acting out of sorrow for sins that spoil God's world.

We will leave behind prejudice and meanness of spirit;
we will play our part in the kingdom of your love.

Old Testament reading   Exodus 17:1-7; 20:1-17 or the reading of the day

Look and see that I am God

Look and see that I am God
who once, for my people, rained down food
and brought water from the rock
in the desert.
**Let us hear you when you call,
and trust you as our God.**

I have been wounded, I have been beaten
by those who indulged their unworthy passions.
**Let us hear you when you call,
and trust you as our God.**

Know and see that I am God.
I search hearts, burn up sins,
protect the powerless and care for the needy.
**Let us hear you when you call,
and trust you as our God.**

*Echoes the Great Canon of St Andrew
of Crete, 740*

New Testament reading   Luke 14:25-33; 15:1-7; 15:11-32; 17:1-4; 18:9-14 or the reading of the day

A Proclamation such as 'Come, let us return to God' may be said.

Come, let us return to God

Come, let us return to God
who has torn us and will heal us.
Bind up our wounds and raise us up, O God.
After two days you will revive us
and on the third day will raise us up
that we may live in your presence.
**We will strive to know you, Lord,
your appearing is as sure as the sunrise.**
You will come to us like the showers,
like the spring rains that water the earth.
Bind up our wounds and raise us up, O God.
O, my people, how shall I deal with you?
Your love for me is like the morning dew
that goes early away.
That is why I have sent prophets
to cut through what is false
and have exposed to you my light.
**You desire integrity, not empty rituals.
Bind up our wounds and raise us up, O God.**

Echoes Hosea 6:1–6

There may be teaching, silence, or singing.

Intercessions My Lord and my God,
take from me all that keeps me from you.
My Lord and my God,
give to me all that brings me nearer to you.
My Lord and my God,
**take me away from myself and give me
completely to you.**

*Brother Klaus of Switzerland**

---

* Nicholas of Flue, d.1487. Switzerland's patron saint – a layman, farmer, parent and hermit.

Saving God, by your incarnation and birth
in poverty,
set us free.
By your prayers and self-discipline,
set us free.
By your tender works of mercy,
set us free.
By your struggle for truth and justice,
set us free.
By your nobility in persecution,
set us free.
By your self-giving even in death,
set us free.

Particular needs may be mentioned after each of the following petitions.

Christ of the scars,
into your hands we place the broken and
wounded . . .

Christ of the scars,
into your hands we place the victims of
violence and false accusation . . .

Christ of the scars,
into your hands we place the refugees and the
hungry . . .

Christ of the scars,
into your hands we place these we now
name . . .

Closing **May the Christ who walked on wounded feet, walk with us on the road.**
May the Christ who serves with wounded hands, stretch out our hands to serve.
May the Christ who loves with a wounded heart, open our hearts to love.

Night Prayer

Opening Tonight we seek your face and forsake our empty hours.
Tonight we seek you above all things.

**Lord Jesus Christ, we confess to you
any grudge or complaint we may have
for anyone,
any ill-will or resentment we may feel,
any critical or judgemental spirit.**

In the looming awfulness of your Cross our sins stand out like great stones.
**Strip from us what is not of you,
give us well-being of the soul.**

Psalm Verses from Psalm 6; 38; 51; 90; 102 or 119:145-152

The following or a declaration may be said.

**Loving Saviour, show yourself to us
that knowing you we may love you as warmly in return,
may love you alone, desire you alone,
contemplate you alone by day and night
and keep you always in our thoughts.
May affection for you pervade our hearts.
May attachment to you take possession of us all.
May love of you fill all our senses.
May we know no other love except you who are eternal.
A love so great that the many waters of land and sea will fail to quench it.**

Columbanus

Bible reading   Matthew 16:16-21 or another reading

There may be silence or singing.

Have mercy this night on a surfeited world
which, through grasping, can't be grasped by you.
Have mercy this night on the weak and broken
on the hungry, the homeless and souls without hope.
Have mercy on us and on those we now name . . . *(Concerns may be spoken.)*

Singing such as 'O Saviour God' to the tune of 'Amazing grace'.

O Saviour God, forgive our sins
as now we seek your face.
We look to you, we leave behind
what blinds us to your grace.

Through many journeys you have been
your children's strength above.
Tonight we ask that nought we do
will cancel out your love.

We lay ourselves before you, Lord,
we rest in love divine.
We sleep in hope of glory years
of being for ever thine.

Closing   Great God, in your goodness you protect us
from the snares of evil.
Bring us safely through the night
that we may offer you our prayers at dawn
which enable us to do your will.
For you are loving to all and we give you the glory,
Father, Saviour and Holy Spirit
now and through the ages.

You have framed the warp of our souls;
at last we will rest in you.
We give thanks for the gift of sleep;
but also for the gift of struggle.
Awake, may we watch with you;
asleep, may we rest in peace.

Holy Week
In the steps of the Suffering Christ

Holy Week is the week preceding Easter Day, when Christians throughout the world seek to follow in the steps of Christ through the last, momentous week of his earth-bound life.

The theme of Palm Sunday is recognition by the crowds of Jesus' unique destiny. The theme of Monday is the cleansing of the temple and of ourselves. The theme of Tuesday is teaching about the meaning of Jesus' mission. The theme of Wednesday is the stature of waiting and the beauty of service. The theme of Thursday is Jesus' last farewell supper, his foreboding and betrayal. The theme of Friday is the trial, the beating, the crucifixion and the shudders of creation. The theme of Saturday is the mourners' grief and the vigil by Jesus' tomb.

Morning Prayer

Opening *There may be singing.*

Children sing your praises,
but we have gone our own way.
A donkey gladly bears your weight,
but we have gone our own way.
A thief will cry to you for mercy,
but we have gone our own way.

When you were crucified, O Lord,
you offered your body and blood on behalf
of all:
your body to refashion us,
your blood to wash us.
You gave up your spirit, O Christ,
to bring us to your Father.

From St Andrew of Crete

Sing or say:

**Lord Jesus Christ, Son of God,
have mercy on me, a sinner.**

Psalm Psalm 69:6-18 (Palm Sunday); 130 (Monday);
56 (Tuesday); 40 (Wednesday);
116:11-18 (Thursday)

Sing or say:

**Lord Jesus Christ, Son of God,
have mercy on me, a sinner.**

Old Testament reading Zechariah 9:9-12 (Palm Sunday); Isaiah 50:4-10 (Monday); Isaiah 42:1-9 (Tuesday); Lamentations 1:1-12 (Wednesday); Exodus 12:1-4, 11-14 (Thursday)

You pour out your life for us

O God, when the ride is bumpy
and the world passes us by,
**you pour out your life for us,
right to the very end.**
When we are edged aside
and doors are shut in our face,
**you pour out your life for us,
right to the very end.**

When others are out to get us
and our home is not secure,
**you pour out your life for us,
right to the very end.**
When our lives are but a flicker
in the darkness that encroaches,
**you pour out your life for us,
right to the very end.**

New Testament reading Luke 19:28-40 (Palm Sunday); Luke 19:41-48 (Monday); Luke 20:9-19 (Tuesday); Matthew 26:1-15 (Wednesday); John 13:1-17, 31b-35 (Thursday)

We, too, will praise you

The leaders turned on you,
the crowds turned from you.
**But the children sang to you
and even the stones would have praised you.**
You alone have the words of eternal life;
to whom else could we go?
**The children, the stones, and we, too,
will praise you.**

Intercessions As his greatest trial drew near, Jesus looked upon the city and wept over it, because it did not recognise its salvation.
Open our eyes, that we may weep with you.

After each petition prayers may be offered or there may be silence.

We weep with you for the blindness of pride
that corrodes the dignity of human life . . .
Open our eyes, that we may weep with you.

We weep with you for the mad rush to consume
that tramples down on the earth and its children . . .
Open our eyes, that we may weep with you.

We weep with you for the lust to control that imprisons the soul and fragments community . . .
Open our eyes, that we may weep with you.

There may be free prayer, silence and singing.

Closing Father, in the life of Jesus you have shown us the way.
Give us his spirit of self-discipline; lead us more deeply into the way of the cross.

Before his hands were stretched out on the cross, they were stretched out in love to children, women, and men.
May your way of the cross be our way, that we, too, may stretch out our hands in love to all.

Midday Prayer

Opening *There may be chant or song.*

Lord, today you teach us.
Your words hold the truth about us and this world.
Yet even as you speak, some slip away from you
to impose their agendas on the world.

Lord, have mercy on us.
Christ, have mercy on us.
Lord, have mercy on us.

Lord, some remain faithful to you.
We, too, would be faithful, even when times are bleak and hope grows dim.

Lord, have mercy on us.
Christ, have mercy on us.
Lord, have mercy on us.

Lord, you warn us: Unless you take up your cross and follow me, you cannot be my disciple.

Lord, have mercy on us.
Christ, have mercy on us.
Lord, have mercy on us.

Lord, you promise us: Unless a grain of wheat falls into the ground and dies, it cannot bear fruit, but if it falls into the ground it will bear much fruit.

Lord, have mercy on us.
Christ, have mercy on us.
Lord, have mercy on us.

Psalm Psalm 119:137-152 or 129

Chant or music.

New Testament reading Romans 15:1-8; Matthew 5:1-12
or the following verse

> Carry each other's burdens, and in this way you will fulfil the law of Christ.
>
> *Galatians 6:2*

**Jesus, master carpenter of Nazareth,
who through wood and nails did win our full salvation,
wield well your tools in this, your workshop,
that we who come to you rough hewn
may here be fashioned to a truer beauty by your hand.**

Silent or spoken reflection.

In the middle of the day we offer to you ourselves, our work and all who are in our hearts.

Prayers may be offered aloud or silently.

There may be music, chant or song.

Saviour of the world, by your Cross and precious death you have redeemed us;
save us and help us, we humbly beseech you, O Lord.

Closing May we carry your cross in our hearts through this day.
**Your cross be in our eyes and in our looking.
Your cross be in our mouths and in our speaking.
Your cross be in our hands and in our working.
Your cross be in our minds and in our thinking.**

Evening Prayer

Opening The One who created us comes willingly to suffer for us;
let us spread our resolves before him like branches of palm.
The Almighty comes to us as one gentle and lowly of heart;
let us put on clothes of humility and praise.
The spirit is willing but the flesh is weak;
let us watch and wait with him.

There may be chanting, music, silence and candle-lighting.

Psalm Psalm 118:15-27 (Palm Sunday); 26 (Monday); 35:11-16 (Tuesday); 102:1-11 (Wednesday); 43 (Thursday)

Forgiveness *The following chant may be said or sung.*

**Lord Jesus Christ, Son of God,
have mercy upon me, a sinner.**

Or the following may be said:

O Saviour of the human race,
O true physician of every disease,
O heart-pitier and assister of all misery,
O fount of true purity and knowledge,
forgive us.

O star-like sun,
O guiding light,
O home of the planets,
O fiery-maned and marvellous one,
forgive us.

O holy scholar of holy strength,
O overflowing, loving, silent one,
O generous and thunderous giver of gifts,
O rock-like warrior of a hundred hosts,
forgive us.
Attributed to St Ciaran, adapted by Ray Simpson

Old Testament reading Isaiah 5:1-7 (Palm Sunday); Lamentations 3:19-33 (Monday); Isaiah 42:1-7 (Tuesday); Jeremiah 7:21-28 (Wednesday); Exodus 11 (Thursday)

There may be silence or the Declaration, 'Jesus, Saviour of the world' (see Declarations, page 156).

New Testament reading Mark 11:1-11 (Palm Sunday); Luke 22:1-38 (Monday); Mark 11:27–13:2 (Tuesday); Mark 14:1-11 (Wednesday); John 13:1-14 (Thursday)

We seek to share your tears

Jesus wept over the city and cried, 'Come to me all you who have burdens.'
We come to you, Lord. To whom else can we go?

Jesus said, 'Can you be baptised with
the baptism
I must be baptised with?'
Lord, we seek to feel your sadness, we seek to share your tears.

There may be teaching, activity, silence or singing.

Intercessions O Christ, take from our hearts the sins that drive us from you.
Help us to remain at one with you.

You saw a widow give what she had;
help us to give our money with love.
You taught us to work like those who tend vines;
help us to tend the planet with love.
You taught that the poor are your family;
help us to serve the poor with love.
Through your defenceless love,
teach us the grace of self-offering.
Through your weakness,
teach us the grace of acceptance.
In your betrayal,
teach us the grace of forgiveness.
In your trials,
teach us the grace of trust.

There may be free prayer and singing.

Closing May the Christ who walked on wounded feet, walk with us on the road.
May the Christ who serves with wounded hands, stretch out our hands to serve.
May the Christ who loves with a wounded heart, open our hearts to love.

Night Prayer

Opening Our desire is to do your will, O God,
our desire is to do your will.
**Our frames are tired and our souls are bowed,
yet still we desire your will.**

In the dark night of the soul we cry out to you.
**Our strength and our friends may fall away,
yet still we cry out to you.**

Psalm Psalm 3 or 10:1-11

There may be silence or music.

You are our Saviour and Lord,
in our stumbling be our Shield,
in our tiredness be our Rest,
in our darkness be our Light.

New Testament reading Jesus said, 'You who kill the prophets and stone those sent to you, how often I have longed to gather you to me as a mother hen gathers her chicks under her wings, but you were not willing.'

Luke 13:34

Intercessions Christ forsaken;
have mercy on all who are forsaken.
Christ afraid;
have mercy on all who are afraid.
Christ betrayed;
have mercy on all who are betrayed.
Christ unnoticed;
have mercy on all who are unnoticed.

We pray for your dear ones and ours, whom you long to gather to you . . . *(names may be mentioned).*

There may be singing.

I place my soul and body
under your guiding this night, O Christ.
**O Son of the journey through darkness,
may your cross this night be my shield.**

Closing We make the sign of the cross of Christ
(make sign),
O Christ of the dying and of deathless love.
**Your cross be between us and all things fearful.
Your cross be between us and all things coming darkly towards us.
Your cross be our sure way from earth to heaven.**

Prayers and Readings for a Thursday Service or Vigil in Holy Week

Readings Psalm
Psalm 4:7-12; 39; 77:1-12; 103:6-18; 116:12-18

Old Testament
Exodus 12:1-8, 11-14; Jeremiah 31:31-34

New Testament
Mark 14:12-26; 1 Corinthians 11:23-32; John 13:1-15

Prayers Today Jesus shares his last Passover Supper with his friends. Today he washes their feet and calls them to love as he loves, even to lay down their lives. Today he is betrayed by his friend, and wracked by the weight of impending gloom. Today he prays that we will unite ourselves around him.

Jesus says to his friends: My heart is breaking with grief, stay with me, watch with me and pray with me.
Lord, we will stay with you, we will watch with you, we will pray with you.

Anguish and dismay came over Jesus. He fell prostrate to the ground, and he prayed:
My heart is breaking with grief, stay with me, watch with me and pray with me.
Lord, we will stay with you, we will watch with you, we will pray with you.

Later Jesus said: Now my hour has come. The Son of humankind is betrayed into the hands of sinful people. My heart is breaking with grief, stay with me, watch with me and pray with me.

Lord, we will stay with you, we will watch with you, we will pray with you.

Today the shadow of greed fell upon the ungodly Judas and he handed over, you, the just judge of all, to unjust judges intent on their own ends.

See how love of money destroys what is good.
See how, because of money, the betrayer hangs himself
and the Creator is led captive to the slaughter.

Lord, have mercy.
Christ, have mercy.
Lord, have mercy.

Father, look upon your family, for whom our Lord Jesus Christ was willing to undergo betrayal and torture. Forgive our unfaithfulness.
Cure us of our sins.
Restore our unity.
Strengthen us to walk the way of the cross.
Bring us to the place of resurrection.

The Jesus Prayer may be repeated ten, twenty or fifty times.

Lord Jesus Christ, Son of God, have mercy upon me, a sinner.

The angel passed over the homes of the God-followers.
The fleeing people passed over the sea.
In their extremity you reached down to them, Lord.
Blessed be the God of eternal covenant.

The Christ walked the land doing works of mercy.

The tyrants dragged him to the gate of death.
In his extremity he called out to you and you heard him.
Blessed be the God of eternal covenant.

O Christ, help us to become one with you.
**In your weakness, teach us the grace of acceptance.
In your betrayal, teach us the grace of forgiveness.
In your trials, teach us the grace of trust.
In your defenceless love, teach us the grace of self-giving.**

Before a Night Vigil on Thursday of Holy Week

Tonight our hearts are heavy.
Our Christ has given love exquisitely.
In his tiredness he has washed the tired feet of his friends.
In his generosity he has given bread to his betrayer.
In his prophetic provision he has, with bread and wine, bequeathed a sacrament that makes him always present to us.
In his prayers he has placed the church of every time and place into the Divine heart.
In his bitter anguish in the garden he has fought with demons and with doubt.
He has been led away captive, to be mocked and tried.
He will not sleep this night
and he calls us to watch and pray.
He said, I give you a new command: Love one another. As I have loved you, so you must love one another. No one has greater love than to lay down their lives for another.
**Jesus, we love you.
We will lay down our lives for one another.**

Prayers and Readings for Good Friday

A wooden cross may be placed in view of everyone.

Readings   Isaiah 53:10-12; Hebrews 4:14-16; 5:7-9; John 18:12–19:37

Reproaches   'The Imagined Reproaches of the Eternal Son of God to the People of the World' may be said – 'My People, what wrong have I done to you?' *(see Declarations, page 157)*

Prayers   Hail! life-giving cross,
when all creation saw you,
all things' Maker and Creator,
hang naked on the cross,
it was changed by fear and wailed.
The sun's light failed and the earth quaked.
The rocks were rent
and temple's veil was rent in two.
The dead were raised from their tombs,
and the powers of heaven cried out in astonishment:
How amazing this is!
The Judge is judged,
he wills to suffer death,
to heal and renew the world.

From an Orthodox Great Vespers

O King of the Friday,
whose limbs were stretched on the cross,
O Lord who did suffer
the bruises, the wounds, the loss.
We stretch ourselves beneath the shield of your might;
some fruit from the tree of your passion
fall on us this night!

Ancient Irish Prayer, anon.

Prayers and Readings for Easter Eve Saturday in Holy Week

In the Celtic Christian tradition it is important to stay with the body of a deceased person, to be with them as they pass over from one mode of existence to another; to focus intently on memories and to offer symbols of devotion such as anointing oils. This applies supremely to the remembrance of Christ's death. Therefore normal activities should be reduced as much as possible on this day, and spaces made to do these things.

This is also the day when Christ visited the world of the dead in order to release spirits still in chains.

The visual focus of this day might be two branches of a tree stripped of its leaves, shaped as a cross, or an icon of Christ descending into the world of the dead.

Tokens of devotion might include flowers, incense and candles.

In the evening it is common to gather for a vigil in darkness or dimmed light. During this there may be biblical readings of dark moments in human history that were followed by promise of God's covenant; these may be interspersed by silence, singing, prayers, poems and storytelling. The following biblical passages may be read or told as stories: Genesis 1:1-5, 26-end; Genesis 7:1-5, 10-18; 9:8-13; Genesis 22:1, 2, 9-13, 15-18; Exodus 14:15-15:1a; Ezekiel 37:1-14.

Baptism vows may be renewed as part of a vigil or church service.

Readings Psalm 53; 60:1-5; 90; 141
Job 14:1-14; 19:24-27
Matthew 27:57-66; 1 Peter 3:18-22

Prayers Today a grave holds him
who holds creation in his hand.
A gravestone covers him
who covers the heavens with glory.
Life sleeps. Hell trembles.
The human race waits with bated breath.

**We have been buried with Christ through baptism.
In faith we will journey with him into dark and unknown places.**

He who holds all things together
was lifted up on the cross
and all creation lamented.
The sun hid its rays.
The stars withheld their light.
The earth shook in fear.
The seas fled and the rocks were split.
Tombs were opened.
The bodies of holy people were raised.
The nether world groaned.
The authorities spread a false report
about Christ's resurrection.
All creation waits with bated breath.

**We have been buried with Christ through baptism.
In faith we will journey with him into dark and unknown places.**

To be read by two people:

First We bless Joseph who came to the Governor by night and asked for the Life of all to be laid in his garden of graves.

Second We bless you for Mary who with sorrow wept as she saw her son hanging on the tree. Her heart was pierced with a sword, as the prophet Simeon had foretold.

First We bless you for the women, who went to the grave to watch, to weep and offer fragrant spices of devotion.

We too, will watch and weep and offer our devotion.

Let us recall what was said about the One whom we mourn:

To be read by eight people:

First No one ever loved as he loved.

Second Someone might lay down their life for a person who did them good: but he laid down his life for those who did him only harm.

Third No one spoke as he spoke. He spoke with authority.

Fourth He knew what was within people.

Fifth We observed him, he was full of grace and truth.

Sixth We were drawn to him because he alone had the words of eternal life.

Seventh He was the voice of the poor, of the dispossessed, who cried, 'Come to me, all you who are loaded with heavy burdens.'

Eighth He cried over our city, 'How often I would have gathered you to me as a hen gathers her chicks, but you would not heed me. Now it is too late.'

We mourn a life of such goodness, cut down in its flower.
We mourn for a people who forfeited the flowering of their destiny.

We mourn for a planet which rejected its Maker.
We mourn for ourselves who languish alone.

Christ, you go forth on your journey.
The mortal shall be clothed with the immortal.
The perishable shall be clothed with the imperishable.

All flesh shall see it.
The spirits of the dead shall be raised.
We shall all be changed.
Christ, go forth on your journey.

This is the night when you saved our forebears from their slavery and led them dry-shod through the sea.
This is the night when Christ broke the chains of sin and death and rose triumphant from the grave.
This is the night when Christians everywhere, washed clean of sin and freed from all that degrades them, are restored to grace.
O Christ, you go through the grave and the gates of death,
open to us the gate of glory.

If there is a silent vigil throughout the night, worshippers may gather around a bier with four large candlestands in dimmed light with a large bowl of incense in front of it. People are invited to restock it throughout the night as needed.

People place cards, flowers, scents or artifacts on or around the bier.

Some traditions celebrate the passing over of Christ from the darkness of death to the light of resurrection as the climax of a vigil. People may gather around a fire outdoors. A large Easter candle which represents the risen Christ may be lit at the fire. The people sing chants or songs as they return to the place of worship.

Easter

Easter celebrates Christ's resurrection from the dead and is the church's greatest festival. It continues for fifty days after Easter Sunday, although Ascension-tide services may be used for any of the last ten days.

An Easter Candle-lighting

A candle is lit.

Jesus Christ is the Light of world;
a light that no darkness can quench.

The long reign of sin has ended.
A new age has dawned.
A broken world is being renewed.
And we are once again made whole.
Alleluia!

Risen Christ, you turned Mary's tears into joy;
turn our tears into joy.
Risen Christ, you turned the travellers' despair into hope;
turn our despair into hope.
Risen Christ, you turned the disciples' fears into boldness;
turn our fears into boldness.
Risen Christ, you turned an empty catch into fullness;
turn our empty chores into fullness.
Risen Christ, you turned Thomas' unbelief into trust;
turn our unbelief into trust.

Scatter the darkness of our unbelief
and shine among us always.
Amen.

An Easter Day Sunrise Service

The service takes place in the open air and begins shortly before sunrise. People gather in silence, facing east whence the sun will rise, where an Easter garden with empty tomb or a cross may be placed.

As the women who first witnessed Jesus' resurrection brought spices early in the morning to adorn his body in the garden tomb, so may we bring hearts of devotion. Some may wish to place a palm cross or a flower before the cross. Let us listen to the sounds of nature. May the birds' chorus be for us a welcome to Christ, whom the Bible calls the Morning Star, and whom the Celtic Church called the Bough of Creation. Because this act of worship is in this spirit, it is sometimes felt inappropriate to have any accoutrements in worship other than the pure voice.

Opening Sleeper, awake, rise from the dead.
Light will shine upon you, Jesus Christ.
Alleluia!

There may be singing.

Reading Luke 24:1-12 or John 20:11-18

Christ is risen!
He is risen indeed! Alleluia!

Rejoice, heavenly powers! Sing, choirs of angels!
Exult, all creation around God's throne:
Jesus Christ, High King of heaven, is risen!
Sound the trumpet of salvation!
Alleluia!

Rejoice, O earth, in shining splendour,
radiant in the brightness of your King!
Christ has conquered death! Glory fills you!
Darkness vanishes for ever!
Alleluia!

Rejoice, O church! Exult in glory! The risen Saviour shines upon you! May this place resound with joy, echoing the mighty song of all God's people! Alleluia!

There may be singing.

Reading   Matthew 28:2-6

Read by two people:

First   Living Lord, come to us in your risen power and make us glad with your presence.

Second   Risen Lord, as Mary Magdalen met you by the garden tomb on the morning of your resurrection, so may we meet you today and every day. Speak to us as you spoke to her. Reveal yourself to us as our living Master. Renew our hope, kindle our joy, and inspire us to share the good news with others.

There may be singing, brief words of encouragement or teaching.

Christ was killed and rose again at the time of the Jewish Passover festival in order to fulfil its meaning: a crossing over. The ancient Jews crossed over from a life of slavery to the land of promise; Jesus crossed over from death to life. We cross over from the slavery and death of sin to the freedom and life of Christ. That is the meaning of our baptism. Let us who are

baptised make an act of unity with the
crucified and risen Christ, so that this becomes
the pattern of our lives.

So let us celebrate, but not with food that
grows stale and decays.
We will celebrate eternal life and truth.

Christ once raised from the dead dies no more:
death has no more power over him.
He died to the self-willed human life;
rising, he lives to God for ever.

Now we too will be dead to sin
and alive to God through Christ our Lord.
Christ has been raised up from the dead:
the first-fruit of those who 'sleep'.

For as by a human death sets in,
by a human comes resurrection of the dead.
For as in Adam all die:
so in Christ shall all be made alive.

We welcome the sun that lights up day:
**we welcome the True Sun who dispels the
shades of sin.**

The sun rises daily only because you
command it;
**its splendour will not last, created things
all perish.**

Christ the true Sun nothing can destroy;
the Splendour of God, he shall reign for ever!

In the light of the risen Christ, all is
transformed. Now we may look back over the
past, we may look in upon our ourselves and
we may look out upon the world, and see all
in a fresh light. We see people and we pray

with the 'resurrection eyes' of our Lord Jesus.
Let us have a time of prayer.

There may be silence, free prayer, or prepared thanksgivings followed by intercessions. This may conclude with everyone saying the Lord's Prayer together. More singing may follow.

Closing Christ is risen! Alleluia!
He is risen indeed! Alleluia!

Listen to the word from God: 'Go quickly and tell the others "He is raised from the dead and is going before you."'
May we walk in the light of your presence.

The risen Christ said: 'My peace I give you.'
Let us give one another a sign of this gift and go in the peace of Christ.
Thanks be to God. Alleluia!

*All may give one another a sign of peace.
Breakfast and flower activities may follow.*

Morning Prayer

Opening Rising from death, today Christ greets his people.
Rising with all creation, we greet you as our King.

Singing, music or a psalm

Let us recollect the presence of the Risen Christ with us now.

Short silence

Forgiveness Christ Jesus, in the light of your risen presence, and in union with your first frail apostles, we say sorry:
**for not weighing your words,
for not sharing your trials,
for not believing your promises.**

Things for which we are sorry may be recalled aloud or in silence.

Risen Christ,
disperse the sin from our souls as the mist departs from the hills.
Be in what we do, inform what we say, redeem who we are.
Amen.

Old Testament reading Isaiah 35

There may be singing or silence.

I am the Resurrection

Jesus says:
I am the resurrection and the life.
You break the power of sin and death.

I am the bread of life.
You feed and fill the hungry.
I am the true vine.
You bring us life eternal.

New Testament reading   Colossians 3:9-17
or another New Testament reading

Silence

We believe, O God of all gods *(see Declarations, page 159)*

Silence or singing

Intercessions   Thank you for bringing us out of the shadow of death;
keep us from falling into sin.

Through the resurrection of your Son you overcame
the hold of sin and death;
transform us in all our ways.

Risen Christ, bring newness of life
**into our stale routines,
into our wearied spirits,
into our tarnished relationships.**

The following themes may be used as headings for extended intercessions.

We pray for believers;
may their lives be signs of joyful service.

We pray that our churches may bring honour to you;
and healing to the people.

We pray for people in authority;
may they strive for justice and peace.

We pray for our communities;
may refreshment be found by all who work.

We pray for our homes;
may they be places of hospitality and hope.

There may be singing.

Closing The God of life go with us.
The Risen Christ beside us.
The vibrant Spirit within us.

Midday Prayer

Opening Christ is risen.
He is risen indeed. Alleluia!
Jesus Christ is the Light of the world.
A light no darkness can quench.
Jesus, rising in glory, scatter the darkness from our paths.
Alleluia!

Risen Christ,
you burst from the grave;
help us to burst into life.
You breathed on your disciples;
breathe your life into us.

Psalm Psalm 30:1-5

Singing or music.

Risen Christ,
you revealed yourself to Mary in the garden at dawn;
reveal yourself to us in the dawnings of our lives.

You revealed yourself to the fisherfolk as they toiled in vain at their work;
reveal yourself to us in the long hours of our toil.

You revealed yourself to the walkers as they welcomed you into their home;
reveal yourself to us as we walk and make welcome our homes.

You revealed yourself to Thomas when he felt the scars in your body;
reveal yourself to us when we touch the scars of the world.

You revealed yourself to many as they met
beneath the skies;
reveal yourself to us in the wonder of your creation.

Free prayer or activity.

New Testament reading The risen Christ said: I am with you always.
                        Matthew 28:20

Silence or singing.

Risen Christ of the miraculous catching of fish,
be with us as we work.
Risen Christ of the perfect lakeside meal,
be with us as we eat.
Risen Christ, of the workaday life
make this a day of joy and peace.

Closing May we
**look upon others with your resurrection eyes,
serve others with your lightness of touch,
and know your well-being in the depths of our soul.**

The Risen Christ be with us
to help us do all things well.

Evening Prayer

Opening Spirit of the Risen Christ,
as the lamps light up the evening,
shine into our hearts and kindle in us the fire
of your love.

An Easter Candle-lighting (see page 95).

Psalm Psalm 66 or the psalm of the day

This may be followed by silence.

We offer to you, Lord, the concerns of this day;
we lay down our burdens at your feet.
**Forgive us our sins, give us your peace,
and help us to receive your Word.
In the name of Christ. Amen.**

Old Testament reading Isaiah 55:8-13

There may be singing.

Thanksgiving We give you thanks, our Provider,
that you are always present, in all things,
each day and each night.
We give you thanks for your gifts of creation,
life and friendship.
We give you thanks for the particular
blessings of this day . . .

There may be a brief pause; sharing of what God has done for us or the naming of blessings.

New Testament reading John 20:1-18

Come, let us return to God *(see page 70)*

Silent reflection, teaching or singing.

Intercessions *There may be free prayer where indicated (. . .).*

Risen Christ, into your hands we place our families, our neighbours, our brothers and sisters in Christ, and all whom we have met today . . .
Enfold them in your will.

Risen Christ, into your hands we place all who are victims of prejudice, oppression or neglect; the frail, the unwanted . . .
May everyone be cherished from conception to the grave.

Risen Christ, into your hands we place all who are restless, sick, or prey to the powers of evil . . .
Tenderly watch over them.

Risen Christ, bring renewal to the land and to the church; to ordained ministries and to religious communities.
Raise up new callings and communities that meet the need of our times.

There may be singing.

Closing Lord Jesus Christ, Light of the world,
by your cross you have overcome all darkness that oppresses.
Come and shine on us here
that we may grow and live together in
your love
which makes us one with all humanity.

The grace of our Lord Jesus Christ, the love of God, and the fellowship of the Holy Spirit be with us all evermore. Amen.

Night Prayer

Opening We come into the presence of the joyful Birther,
we come into the presence of the rising Son.
We come into the presence of the life-giving Spirit,
we come into the presence of the Three-in-One.

We rejoice in the day when Christ rose again.
We will lie down in his joy and peace!

Psalm Psalm 118:15-24, or 126, or verses from the psalm for the day

This night, O Victor over death:
raise us from the death of denial,
raise us from the death of fear,
raise us from the death of despair.

This night, O Victor over death:
wake us to the eternal 'Yes',
wake us to the rays of Hope,
wake us to the light of Dawn.

There may be singing or music.

New Testament reading John 20:19, 20; 1 Peter 3:18, 22; 2 Corinthians 4:11-16 or another New Testament reading

We lie down in peace knowing our sins are forgiven;
we lie down in peace knowing death has no fear.
We lie down in peace knowing no powers can harm us;
we lie down in peace knowing angels are near.

Risen Christ of the scars, who spoke peace to your desolate disciples,
speak peace this night to us and to desolate ones we love.
We remember these and others that we love . . .
(*Any may mention names.*)

Risen Christ of the lakeside, who nourished and inspired your disciples, inspire us and these your loved ones to rest this night in your presence.

There may be silence, singing or music.

Closing Risen Christ, watch over us this night
and keep us in the light of your presence.
May our praise continually blend
with the song of all creation.

**Deep peace of the setting sun,
deep peace of the forgiving heart,
deep peace of the lakeside Christ
be ours, tonight, for ever.**

The eye of the Risen Christ be upon us as we sleep;
the eye of affection and mercy,
the eye of joy and gladness,
bringing to dawn our wholeness.

Ascension

This begins on the Thursday ten days before Pentecost Sunday. It marks the last of the forty days the physically resurrected Christ spent on earth, his farewell and his final commission.

As Christians have reflected upon this event, they have realised its significance for the whole human race. Christ, as the representative of the human race, has taken humanity into the heart of God.

Jesus called his followers to spend the days following his physical disappearance waiting on God, in order to receive the Holy Spirit, or Power, which God would send them.

Morning Prayer

Opening Christ is risen!
He is risen indeed. Alleluia!
Christ has ascended!
Our High King – He shall reign for ever.
In love of the King of Life we shall celebrate.
Alleluia!

There may be singing.

Psalm Psalm 92; 104; 110; 117; 139; 147:1-12; 148; 149 or 150

The following Proclamation or 'The Song of Christ's Glory' may be said (see Declarations, page 160).

Trumpets of the earth proclaim,
Christ who once in earth had lain,
goes in triumph now to reign.
Alleluia!

He sits with God upon his throne,
the Father's glory is his own,
he the eternal, radiant Son.
Alleluia!

All human life with him is raised,
the weakest ones by heaven are praised,
now high and low on him have gazed.
Alleluia!

Old Testament reading 2 Kings 2:1-15 or the reading of the day

High King,
you are crowned with glory.

Victor in the race,
you call us to follow you.

High Priest,
you understand our every need.

Eternal Giver,
you shower your gifts on every soul.

Head of the church,
you wish no one to be separate from your Body.

Sender,
you promise us your Holy Spirit.

New Testament reading Luke 24:50-53; Acts 1:1-11; Matthew 28:16-20; or 1 Peter 2:4-10

There may be the Declaration 'The Song of Christ's Glory' (see Declarations, page 160) or creed, silent meditation, teaching or singing.

ASCENSION

Intercessions Sovereign of the Universe,
a cloud hid you from sight
yet your mortal humanity has been raised to life in God.

We pray for those whose life is clouded:
raise them to life in you.

For those clouded by fear:
raise them to life in you.

For those clouded by worry:
raise them to life in you.

For those clouded by hostility:
raise them to life in you.

May tiny infants in the womb be raised to life in you;
may the handicapped and ailing be raised to life in you;
may bronzed and brave adventurers be raised to life in you;
may thinkers and researchers be raised to life in you;
may the battle-scarred and weary be raised to life in you.
May the whole human family be raised to life in you.

There may be silence, free prayer or singing.

Closing May the King of glory fill you with joy, make you expectant, keep you in unity, and bring you the Power from on high.
Alleluia!

Midday Prayer

Opening Jesus, you embraced our humanity and took it into the heart of God.
Alleluia!

You clothe human life in unfading dignity.
Alleluia!

Now we will revere you in all we do,
discern you in every place
and love you in each person we meet.
Alleluia!

New Testament reading He who descended into the world below also ascended far above the heavens in order that he might fill all things and give gifts to his people ... that we might come to maturity, to our full stature in Christ.

Ephesians 4:10, 11

To be read by three people:

First   You came down,
to lift us up.

Second   You descended to earth,
that earth might ascend to heaven.

Third   You descended to the dead,
that the dead might rise to life.

First   In the heat of the day,
lift us up.

Second   In our fretting cares,
lift us up.

Third   In our difficulties,
lift us up.

First   In our tiredness,
lift us up.

ASCENSION

Second In disappointment,
lift us up.

Any In . . .
lift us up.

Lift us Lord,
**out of darkness into light,
out of despair into hope.**

Lift us, Lord,
**out of sadness into joy,
out of failure into trust.**

Lift us, Lord,
**out of anger into forgiveness,
out of pride into freedom.**

There may be singing.

Psalm Psalm 121

There may be silence.

O Lord, you are very great.
You are clothed with honour and majesty,
you are wrapped in light as with a garment.
You can do immeasurably more than we can ask or imagine by the power which is at work in us.
We give glory to you through the ages of ages.
Amen.

Ascended King, your kingdom come, your will be done, on earth as it is in heaven.

There may be free prayer as follows.

Your kingdom come in . . . *(Places or persons may be named.)*

There may be singing or music.

**Yours, Lord, is the greatness, the power,
the glory**
the splendour and the majesty.
Everything in heaven and earth is yours.
All things come from you, and of your own
do we give you.

Closing May the Eternal Glory shine upon us,
may the Son of Mary stay beside us,
may the life-giving Spirit work within us,
now and through the ages. Amen.

ASCENSION

Evening Prayer

Opening Christ departs,
but Love's fragrance ever lingers.
Death is conquered;
fear has lost its power.
A human heart now lives in God;
the fullness we long for we shall now receive.

There may be singing.

Psalm Psalm 24; 93; 97 or 98

Ascended Lord, you have made us living stones of the temple you are to build.
We offer all that we are and all that we have to you.
King of Glory:
ennoble us.
King of Grace:
cherish us.
King of Life:
renew us.
King of Promise:
surprise us.

Old Testament reading Isaiah 52:7-12 or the reading of the day

The Song of Christ's glory *(see Declarations, page 160)*

New Testament reading Matthew 28:16-20 or the reading of the day

Promised Spirit

Promised Spirit,
come as the dew in the night,
come as the rain on dry land,
come as the fire in hours of cold,
come to renew in us your image of love.

There may be teaching and singing.

Intercessions Ascended Lord, you call those who follow you
to a time of waiting,
that they may be able to receive the gifts you
delight to shower on your church,
and to receive the empowering Spirit.
Take from us obstinate ways.
Give us receptive hearts.
Make us fertile ground.

There may be silence or music.

Lord, before you left this earth, you urged your
friends to immerse all peoples in your life.
We pray for parched and hungry people;
immerse them in your life.
We pray for torn and exiled people;
immerse them in your life.
We pray for lonely and unloved people;
immerse them in your life.
We pray for unjust and oppressive people;
immerse them in your life.

There may be free prayer and singing.

Closing The grace of our Lord Jesus Christ, the love
of God and the fellowship of the Holy Spirit
be with us all, evermore. Amen.

ASCENSION

Night Prayer

Opening Ancient legend says that before Christ left the earth he told his disciples:
I have no hands but yours, I have no eyes but yours, I have no lips but yours, I have no feet but yours.

As we go to rest we offer ourselves to you, Lord;
may our hands be your hands,
may our eyes be your eyes,
may our lips be your lips,
may our feet be your feet.

Reading Psalm 113

There may be silence or singing.

The One who once was crowned with thorns
is now crowned with glory.
The One who descended to the depths now
lifts us to himself.
Lord, lift us up.

We pray for the down-trodden and destitute.
Lord, lift them up.

We pray for the deserted and despairing.
Lord, lift them up.

We pray for our loved ones.
Lord, lift them up.

Let us pray, aloud or silently, for people on our hearts . . .

New Testament reading John 16:28; Ephesians 4:7-13; Hebrews 10:12-14; 1 Peter 3:18-22 or say 'The Song of Christ's Glory' *(see Declarations, page 160)*

Prepare us to receive the Spirit of Christ;
the Spirit of wisdom, strength and joy.

There may be silence, singing or music.

Intercessions Great God, as the haze rises from mountain tops,
raise our souls from the granite of death
before we go to sleep.

As we lay down our clothes,
may we lay down our struggles
before we go to sleep.

Lift from us our anguish,
lift from us our empty pride
before we go to sleep.

Give us grace,
give us joy
before we go to sleep.

Closing May the crowned King hold a crown over us,
may the Eternal Glory shine light upon us,
may the Power from on high overshadow us
as we sleep.

Pentecost
Walking in the Spirit

This begins fifty days after Jesus' resurrection and celebrates the coming of the Holy Spirit. In Celtic tradition this is a forty day period of 'walking in the Spirit' during which these worship patterns are especially suitable.

Morning Prayer

Opening Creator Spirit, come,
fresh as the morning dew.
**Inflaming Spirit, come,
kindle our hearts anew.**

There may be singing.

Psalm Psalm 36:5-9; 139:7-12; 23 or 24

A Song of the Spirit

I will gather you from the nations,
I will sprinkle pure water upon you and cleanse you from all that defiles,
I will put a new spirit within you and you shall be my people.
A new heart I will give you,
I will remove your heart of stone and give you a heart of flesh,
I will put a new spirit within you and you shall be my people.
You shall be my people and I shall be your God.
Glory to the Source, Creator, Redeemer and ever-flowing Spirit.

Verses from the Book of Ezekiel

Old Testament reading   Ezekiel 37:1-14; Jeremiah 31:31-34; Joel 2:28, 29 or the reading of the day

Spirit of the quiet earth,
Spirit breathing hope to birth,
bring forth in us the fruit of love.
Spirit, kindle flame that darts,
Spirit, waken song in hearts.

Spirit blowing through creation,
inspiring deeds for proclamation,
bring forth in us the fruit of life.
Spirit, kindle flame that darts,
Spirit, waken song in hearts.

Spirit tearing down our walls,
be the One who speaks and calls,
bring forth in us the fruit of faith.
Spirit, kindle flame that darts,
Spirit, waken song in hearts.

New Testament reading   The extract below; John 16:4b-15; Acts 2:1-11, 4:23-31 or the reading of the day

When Pentecost came the disciples
were together
... and there came what looked like tongues
of flame. These separated and rested on the
head of each one individually.

Acts 2:1, 3

Flame of love,
light us up.

Flame of truth,
light us up.

Flame of seeing,
light us up.

There may be singing.

God of the call, God of the journey, you have
anointed your servants from the Day of
Pentecost until now.
Anoint us as you will for the ministries you will.
Here we wait, alert and open, praying that
you will come to us . . .

*Sing 'Come, Holy Spirit' (see Declarations,
page 161) or another song.*

Intercessions *There may be intercessions, silence, music, open
ministry, laying on of hands, singing in the Spirit,
other creative activity or any of the following
prayers may be said.*

Strength-giver,
may your fibre grow in us.
Fortifier,
may your praises swell in us.
Indweller,
may your presence dwell in us.

O Spirit, be free in us,
let us not bind you through fear
of where your disturbing power will lead.
Burst through this brittle shell,
shake us to the foundations,
strip us to the core
which is our essence and your love.

There may be singing.

Closing **The blessing of the perfect Spirit be ours,
the blessing of the Three be pouring on us,
graciously and generously,
hour by hour.**

Midday Prayer

Opening Come from the four winds, mighty Spirit of God, and revive your weary people.

In our labour,
be our Refreshment.

In our adversity,
be our Strength.

In our distress,
be our Comfort.

For your Spirit permeating every atom of creation,
we praise you with wonder in our being.
For your creativity planted deep in every soul,
we praise you with wonder in our being.

In the beginning, O God,
your Spirit swept over the chaos of the cosmos
like a wild wind
and creation was born.
In the deep and unsettled waters of our lives
and our lands today,
let there be new birthings of your Spirit.

New Testament reading Jesus said: If anyone is thirsty, let them come to me and drink. From the heart of the person who believes in me shall flow rivers of living water. He said this about the Spirit, which those who believed in him were to receive.

John 7:37-39

Spirit of the living God, anoint our creativity, ideas and energy, so that even the smallest tasks may bring you honour.

When I am confused,
guide me.
When I am weary,
energise me.
When I am burned out,
infuse me.

Release in us the power of your Spirit
that our souls may be free
to roam your boundless stretches of space.
May we,
soar high like the eagle,
glow like the fire,
flow like a river.

Silent or free prayer and singing.

Psalm   Psalm 46

Closing   The Uncomfortable Blessing

May the Spirit bless you with discomfort at easy answers, half-truths and superficial relationships,
so that you will live deep in your heart.

May the Spirit bless you with anger at injustice and oppression, and exploitation of people and the earth, so that you will work for justice and peace.

May the Spirit bless you with tears to shed for those who suffer, so that you will reach out your hand to comfort them.

And may the Spirit bless you with foolishness to think that you can make a difference in the world,
so that you will do all the things which others say cannot be done.

or

**Great Spirit, Wild Goose of the Almighty,
be our eye in the dark places,
be our flight in the trapped places,
be our host in the wild places,
be our brood in the barren places,
be our formation in the lost places.**

Be with us, Lord, now and for the rest of the day;
**filled with your Spirit, may we journey on
with you.**

Evening Prayer

Opening You led your people by a cloud;
lead us by your Spirit now.
You lit your people by a fire;
light us by your Spirit now.

There may be singing.

Psalm Psalm 104:25-end; 150, or another psalm

Spirit of God,
the breath of creation is yours.
Spirit of God,
the groans of the world are yours.
Spirit of God,
the wonder of communion is yours.
And we are filled.
And we are filled.

There may be silence.

Old Testament reading Exodus 31:1-11; 33:7-11; 1 Samuel 10:1-7 or the reading of the day

May your Spirit cover all
O King of the Tree of life,
the blossoms on the branches are your people,
the singing birds are your angels,
the whispering breeze is your Spirit.

O King of the Tree of Life,
may the blossoms bring forth sweetest fruit,
may the birds sing out the highest praise,
may your Spirit cover all with her gentle breath.

New Testament   Romans 8:22-27; 1 Corinthians 12:4-11
       reading   or the reading of the day

> **Come, like fire, and kindle love in our hearts.**
> **Come, like wind, and breathe life into**
> **our frames.**
> **Come, like water,**
> **and immerse us in your presence.**
> **Come, like earth,**
> **and sustain our being.**

There may be a Creed, teaching, sharing, and singing.

Intercessions   Holy Spirit, fulfil in us the work begun by Jesus.
Invigorate our work,
subdue our pride,
raise us to wonder.

Come, Holy Spirit, shower your gifts upon
your people:
gifts of wisdom and understanding;
gifts of healing and practical help;
gifts of speech and heartfelt tears;
gifts of love which bind us together in peace.

God whose breath gives energy for struggle,
set us free to grow as the children of God:
open our ears
that we may hear the weeping of the world;
open our mouths
that we may be a voice for the voiceless;
open our eyes that we may discern your ways;
open our hearts that we may bring faith to life.

Spirit of God,
among the wheels of industry,
renew the face of the earth.
Among the computers of commerce,
renew the face of the earth.
Among crime-infested neighbourhoods,
renew the face of the earth.
Among tired and broken families,
renew the face of the earth.
Among the lonely and the sick,
renew the face of the earth.
Among the drugged and disillusioned,
renew the face of the earth.
Among . . .
renew the face of the earth.

There may be singing.

Closing As the water in the stream makes its journey to the sea, so may you flow with the Spirit until your life becomes complete.

Night Prayer

Night lights are lit.

Opening When Pentecost came the disciples were together and there came what looked like tongues of flame. These separated and rested on the head of each one individually.

Acts 2:1, 3

Come, flame of love.
Come, flame of truth.
Come, flame of joy.

There may be singing.

Psalm Psalm 139:1-12

As the sun sets,
renew the face of the earth.
Where there are tired and broken people,
renew the face of the earth.
Where night-life breeds disillusion,
renew the face of the earth.
Where those we care for dwell,
whom we name before you now,
renew the face of the earth.
(Names may be mentioned)
As we wait on you now,
renew the face of the earth.

May the Spirit of the Lord rest upon you,
the spirit of wisdom and understanding.

Isaiah 11:2

In silence people kneel or sit with hands open to receive the Spirit. This may be followed by prepared, silent or informal intercessions, sharing, laying on of hands or singing in the Spirit.

Closing The Spirit rest upon your brow,
keep you safe in every hour.
When you wake with work to do,
Holy Spirit, see you through.

Trinity

The heart of God is a communion of three flowing Loves – sending, saving, sustaining. In the Celtic tradition the Trinity is not simply allotted a season in the Church's year but is recognised as the very fabric of its life and worship at all times. Humans are designed to reflect the Trinity from whom flows true community, and a society rooted in good relationships. These prayer patterns may therefore be used at any time, especially from the Sunday after Pentecost until the Angel Season that begins on 29 September.

Morning Prayer

Opening God who is One,
you create us in diversity.
God who is Three,
you draw us into unity.
We give thanks for the Three who are love,
we give thanks for the Three who are here.

There may be singing.

We arise today in a mighty strength;
the God who is One,
the God who is Three,
creating all through love.

We arise today
in the might of the Father,
in the strength of the Son,
in the gentleness of the Spirit,
affirming all through love.

Psalm	Psalm 8; 86:8-13 or the psalm of the day
Forgiveness	We grieve that we who are made to reflect your threefold love have violated our nature and yours. **Holy God, holy and immortal, have mercy upon us.** *Forgiveness of sins may be declared or there may be music or silence.*
Old Testament reading	Exodus 3:1-6, 13-15 or the reading of the day

We bless you for the Triune God

We bless you for the sun:
**its source of fire,
its beams of light,
its rays of warmth.**

We bless you for the water:
**when it is ice,
when it is steam,
when it is flowing free.**

We bless you for the human being:
**the being who thinks,
the being who acts,
the being who feels.**

We bless you for the Triune God:
**the Triune who creates,
the Triune who takes flesh,
the Triune who transforms.**

New Testament reading	John 16:5-15; 17:1-11 or the reading of the day

**Glory to the Father,
glory to the Son,
glory to the Spirit,
ever Three in One.**

Thanksgiving   Power of powers,
we worship you.
Light of lights,
we worship you.
Life of lives,
we worship you.

Source of life,
we turn to you.
Saviour of life,
we turn to you.
Sustainer of life,
we turn to you.

Love before time,
we adore you.
Love in darkest time,
we adore you.
Love in this time,
we adore you.

There may be teaching, sharing, silence, singing.

Intercessions   Father, you bring worlds to birth,
you bring us to birth and you affirm us.
We bring to you unaffirmed places in ourselves
and unaffirmed people in the world . . . *(Pause, or people or aspects of ourselves may be mentioned.)*

Father, affirm them.
Father, affirm them.

Saviour, you reach our brokenness
and make us whole,
you reach those who are alienated
and bring them home.
We pray for broken and alienated people . . .
(Pause, or people or aspects of ourselves may be mentioned.)

Saviour, bring them home.
Saviour, bring them home.

Spirit, you permeate all creation
and renew the springs of life,
we pray for parched and wearied people . . .
*(Pause, or people or aspects of ourselves may be
mentioned.)*

Spirit, renew them.
Spirit, renew them.

*There may be free prayer, the Lord's Prayer and
singing.*

Closing   Eternal God and Father,
you create us by your power
and redeem us by your love:
guide and strengthen us by your Spirit,
that we may give ourselves in love and service
to one another and to you,
through Jesus Christ our Lord.

The following blessing may be said.

**Into the Sacred Three we immerse you,
into their power and peace we place you,
may their breath be yours to live,
may their love be yours to give.
Into the Sacred Three we immerse you.**

Midday Prayer

Opening Love birthing,
we honour you.
Love briding,
we adore you.
Love binding,
we embrace you.

Open our eyes to see you reflected around us.
**In the sun that is fire, light and warmth,
in the water that is steam, ice and drink.**

Old Testament reading God said:
Let us make human beings in our likeness.
Genesis 1:26

Alternate lines of the following may be read by two groups, e.g. male and female, those sitting on left and right.

Thank you for the little trinities that reflect to us your nature.
1 **For lovemaking, conceiving and nurturing.**
2 **For young and old, male and female, making sport and music together.**

New Testament reading The grace of the Lord Jesus Christ, the love of God and the fellowship of the Holy Spirit be with us all. *2 Corinthians 13:13*

There may be shared or silent reflection and music.

God beyond,
glory to you.
God within,
glory to you.
God between,
glory to you.
One God, Source of all being.

In our journeying this day,
keep us, Father, in your way.
In our play and in our work,
guide us, Saviour, by your word.
In our thoughts and in our talk,
may we, Spirit, with you walk.
In our friendships let us be,
in the Blessed Trinity.

There may be free prayer or singing.

Closing   The blessing of the Source be yours.
The blessing of the Saviour be yours.
The blessing of the Spirit be yours.
The blessing of the Three be yours.

**May they pour upon us in mercy
hour by hour.**

TRINITY

Evening Prayer

Opening The Three who are over our head,
the Three who are under our tread,
the Three who are over us here,
the Three who are over us there,
the Three who in heaven do dwell,
the Three in the great ocean swell,
pervading Three, O be with us,
pervading Three, O be with us.

There may be singing.

Psalm Psalm 85, 90, 113, 115, 146, or 147

Faith in the Three

For my shield this day I call:
a mighty power, the Holy Trinity.
Faith in the Three, trust in the One,
creating all through love.

In faith I trust in the Father of all:
he's my refuge, a very strong tower.

For my shield this day I call:
Christ's power in his coming,
Christ's power in his dying,
Christ's power in his rising.

For my shield this day I call:
the mighty Spirit who breathes through all.
Faith in the Three, trust in the One,
making all through love.

Old Testament reading Isaiah 59:15b-21 or the reading of the day

Forgiveness **The Father is always birthing,**
the Saviour is always restoring,
the Spirit is always renewing,
forgive us for failing to reflect them.

A silence, a declaration of forgiveness, mime or music may follow.

New Testament reading Mark 1:1-11 (on Trinity Sunday) or the reading of the day

There may be recital of a Creed, teaching, sharing, creative activity, or singing.

Intercessions Birther, who brought worlds into being,
bring to birth what you purpose for us.

If there is guided or free prayer, pray for good things to be brought to birth.

Saviour, who reconnected an estranged world to its Source,
reconnect us to the Source of our being.

If there is guided or free prayer, pray for estranged facets of God's world to be reconnected.

Spirit, who breathes through everything that lives,
breathe fullness of life into us.

If there is guided or free prayer, pray for withered people and places to be restored to fullness of life.

Triune God, who delights to bring diversity in unity,
bring unity to our diversity.

If there is guided or free prayer, pray for groups and peoples to reflect God's unity in diversity.

Triune God, you call us to reflect your unity in diversity.
We pray for places where community has been destroyed;
may people turn to you, and community grow again.

Closing May the love of the Three give birth to new community,
may the life of the Three give birth to new creativity,
may the oneness of the Three give birth to new unity.

There may be free prayer and singing.

Sacred Three our Friendship be encircling us eternally.

Night Prayer

Opening *Three unlit candles are set in place.*

I light this candle in the name of the Creator
who birthed the world and breathed life into me.

(This or another chant may be sung.)

**Gloria, gloria, gloria,
in excelsis Deo.**

I light this candle in the name of the Saviour
who entered the world and stretched out his
hand to me.

(This or another chant may be sung.)

**Gloria, gloria, gloria,
in excelsis Deo.**

I light this candle in the name of the Spirit
who pervades the world and fills me.

(This or another chant may be sung.)

**Gloria, gloria, gloria,
in excelsis Deo.**

**We will light three lights for the Trinity of love;
God above us,
God beside us,
God beneath us.**

Father, cherish me,
Son, cherish me,
Spirit, cherish me,
Three all-kindly.

**God, make me holy,
Christ, make me holy,
Spirit, make me holy,
Three all-holy.**

Three, aid my hope,
Three, aid my love,
Three, aid my eye,
Three all-knowing.

There may be singing.

Psalm Psalm 104

As I enter into sleep,
keep my soul, O Father, keep.
As I enter into rest,
renew my frame, O Saviour blest.
When I wake with work to do,
Holy Spirit, see me through.
Holy Three, my shield, my wall,
be my rest, my joy, my all.

Our dear ones bless, O God, wherever they are, especially . . .

There may be singing.

Day has ended,
Father, guard us sleeping.
Night has come,
Saviour, guard us sleeping.
Our minds need calm,
Spirit, guard us sleeping.
Look on us, Lord,
Father, guard us sleeping.
Warm us, Lord,
Saviour, guard us sleeping.
We rest in you, Lord,
Spirit, guard us sleeping.

Closing May the blessing of the Son
help you do what must be done.
May the Spirit stroke your brow
as weary down to sleep you go.
May the Father mark your rest
empower you for tomorrow's test.
May the Trinity rekindle
the pure flames of your life's candle.
Ramon Beeching, Pocket Celtic Prayers

Remembrance of Saints

In the western church this season begins with All Saints' Eve (31 October), All Saints' Day (1 November) and All Souls' Day (2 November). In the eastern church All Saints' Day is the first Sunday after Pentecost.

1 November connects with the early British and Irish calendars which marked Samhain, the winter season which began their new year.

Lutherans (like other Protestant traditions) do not celebrate official saints, but observe a general commemoration of the dead on the first Sunday in November. In translating this material, phrases such as 'the cloud of witnesses' and 'role models of Christ' may replace the term 'saints'.

Hallowe'en – All Saints' Eve

Opening *A candle is lit.*

God of eternity, God of the saints, you are:
stronger than the elements,
stronger than the shadows,
stronger than the fears,
stronger than the dark powers that assail us.

Psalm Psalm 11, 16 or 18:1-3

Chant or song.

Old Testament reading   Isaiah 43:1-3a

With Christ, to whom the spirits were subject,
we claim the victory of the Lord.
With the desert Christians, from whom the demons fled,
we claim the victory of the Lord.
With hermits who made wild places safe with prayer,
we claim the victory of the Lord.
With martyrs who vaulted over death,
we claim the victory of the Lord.
With prayer-warriors who overthrew hell's great might,
we claim the victory of the Lord.
With Patrick who freed his land of serpent powers,
we claim the victory of the Lord.
With Brigid who turned fierce strongholds into havens of peace,
we claim the victory of the Lord.
With Cuthbert, healer and conqueror of the dark places,
we claim the victory of the Lord.
With the saints of this place,
we claim the victory of the Lord.

New Testament reading   Matthew 5:1-10; Luke 10:17-24; Philippians 2:6-11; Hebrews 12:1, 2, 22-24; 1 John 3:1-3; Revelation 7:9-17; or Revelation 21:1-8

There may be singing.

Intercessions We place into your hands the places that will be little used in the season of darkness and cold.

**We place into your hands
the season we leave behind
and winter's patterns,
which you call us now to live.**

Silence

Night-lights may be lit inside objects such as a pumpkin and a rock.

May light shine in the bowels of the earth.
May light shine in the ghouls of the air.

Each person may light and hold a candle.

May fears diminish and light increase in the people and places we now name . . . *Names of people and places may be spoken spontaneously or in prayers prepared earlier.*

The shield of Christ be over them,
**the shield of the angels guard them,
the shield of the saints hearten them,
the shield of life eternal.**

Chant or song.

Closing The God of life go with us
**to protect us from ill,
to keep our hearts still,
to strengthen our will.**

People may walk, with their candles, to a place that attracts dark memories or powers, or to a cemetery, to leave prayers or lights.

Rest eternal grant to them, O Lord,
and let light perpetual shine upon them.

Emblems, faces or sayings of saints may be depicted for use at a Hallowe'en party or the following day.

All Saints' Day – The Cloud of Witnesses

For use at any time, especially 1 November, 13 May or the week following Pentecost.

All Christians are called to be saints. In the Celtic tradition, and generally in the early church, a person who had inspired many others to live holy lives was affirmed as a saint at his or her funeral, and was commemorated on the anniversary of their birth into heaven, that is, on the day of their death. Protestants who reject the cult of saints nevertheless welcome as role models people whose witness to Christ still speaks to us.

Christians came to realise the value of celebrating from time to time the whole community of such people, including those about whom not enough is known to warrant a commemoration day of their own.
St Ephrem of Syria (d. 373) encouraged this. By the time of St Chrysostom (d. 407) this celebration was assigned to the first Sunday after Pentecost, and the Eastern Orthodox Church retains this day still. In the west it was celebrated on 13 May but in the eighth century it was transferred to 1 November.

Opening   We arise,
**in the glorious company of the holy and risen ones,
in the prayers of the fathers and mothers,
in the truths of apostles.**

We arise,
**in the innocence of virgins,
in the victory of martyrs,
in the friendship of those in love with the
King of Life.**

In the darkness of this passing age your saints
declare your presence and bring to us
your glory.
Glory to God for ever.

Psalm   Psalm 33:1-5; or 112:1-9

Forgiveness   Welcoming light, loneliness and self-sufficiency
have no place where your friends are
entertained.
**Forgive us for the places where we have shut
them out.**

*There may be silence or an assurance of
forgiveness.*

Old Testament reading   Wisdom 5:14-16 or Jeremiah 31:31-34

Thanksgiving   We thank you that in your saints of yesterday
and today we see the many-splendoured
facets of human life flowing in their fullness.
We thank you for those who
give their all in the service of others,
overcome heroic odds with nobility of spirit,
are gracious in defeat and magnanimous
in triumph,
are content with the little things
and show us how to truly love.
**Spurred on by them we offer you
our talents and our tasks,
our trials and our triumphs.**

or

The response (R) after each line is:
Who shine in the world and light up our way.

We give you thanks for our saints. *(R)*
We give you thanks for the midwives of the faith. *(R)*
We give you thanks for those who fight for equality of regard. *(R)*
We give you thanks for those who seek the dignity of life and labour. *(R)*
We give you thanks for those who are true shepherds of their people. *(R)*
We give you thanks for . . . *(R)*

We give you thanks in union with those who sing the eternal song of victory:
(all say or sing)
**Holy, holy, holy is the Lord,
holy is the Lord God Almighty,
who was, and is, and is to come,
holy, holy, holy is the Lord.**

With John the loved disciple who soars like an eagle *(see Declarations, page 162)*

Singing might include the song 'The Lord will make us strong' (see Declarations, page 163)

New Testament reading Hebrews 12:1, 2 or Revelation 7:9-12

People may offer creative expressions of their devotion, or of the cloud of witnesses and singing.

Intercessions On this day of the saints of life,
**send the dew that makes faith grow strong,
establish in our beings
the law of eternal love.**

On this day of the saints of power,
quell the wrath of the squalls that break,
be with us in the eye of the storm,
your compass in our hearts.

On this day of the saints of virtue,
be with us in our tasks,
heaven's company sharing our work,
bringing us mercy and peace.

Encourage those you call to run their race
with all their heart;
keep us worthy of our calling,
that we may come with your saints
to glory everlasting.

Great God of the saints,
we join our prayers with theirs.
Knit us together with those you have
already called;
hasten the day when we shall be one.

As they shine,
may we shine.
As we walk in their steps,
may we join them in glory everlasting.

Closing God of the waiting ones,
as the saints do in heaven,
may we do on earth:
in using our gifts,
in caring for others,
in holy dying.

Night Prayers

Opening The shield of God be with us this night,
the glorious company of the holy and
risen ones,
the prayers of the fathers and mothers,
the visions of prophets,
the deeds of steadfast believers.

**From dark powers that assail us,
from false words that ensnare us,
from fears that invade us,
the saints in heaven protect us.**

Christ, Son of the living God,
may your holy saints guard our sleep.
May they watch over us as we rest,
and hover around our beds.

**Let them reveal to us in our dreams,
visions of your glorious truth,
may no fears or worries delay
our willing, prompt repose.**

Bible reading Hebrews 12:1, 2; 22-24; Matthew 5:1-10;
1 John 3:1-3; Philippians 2:5-15, or another
Bible reading

There may be singing.

This may be followed by music or by silence during which anyone may give thanks for a saintly person whose memory they value.

Intercessions May the saints and the Saviour watch over our loved ones this night, especially . . .

Anyone may mention names.

May the saints and the Saviour
protect them from the hostile powers,
and put balm into their sleep.

We lie down this night with the Three of Love,
and they will lie down with us.
We lie down this night with the whole company
of heaven,
and they will lie down with us.
God, the saints and the angels,
lying down with us.

Closing With the saints in glory we make the sign of the cross of Christ *(make sign)*.
May your cross come between us and all things harmful;
your cross light up for us the company of heaven.
This night and for ever.

Declarations

We bless you – The song of Zechariah

We bless you, Lord God of Israel,
coming to ransom your people.

**Raising up saving power
in the family of your servant David,
as you said by the mouth of your prophets
in days of old.**

You set us free from oppression,
free from the hands of our foes.
This is your bond of love with our forebears,
your covenant binding for ever.

**Your oath to our father Abraham,
assuring us that, freed from fear,
delivered from all oppression,
we will serve you in goodness and love
to the end of our days.**

This child will be called your prophet,
he will walk in your presence
and prepare the way you will come,
announcing your people's salvation
with pardon for all their sins.

**Through the love in the heart of our God
the Rising Sun will come to us,
shining on those in the dark
who lie in the shadow of death,
and guiding our steps into peace.**

Luke 1:68-79

We wait

With Abraham and Moses,
waiting to be led to a place of promise,
we wait.

With Amos and Hosea, Isaiah, Micah
and all the prophets,
believing that you are a God of justice,
we wait.

With Paul and Silas,
and all God's people imprisoned and
persecuted for acting on their faith,
we wait.

With Naaman and Jairus, Bartimaeus
and the Syro-Phoenician woman,
and all who long for an end to pain and
rejection,
we wait.

With Zacchaeus in his tree,
the Samaritan widow at the well,
and all who yearn to be liberated from a
half-life,
we wait.

With Sarah and Hannah, Elizabeth and Mary,
and all who look forward to new life and
beginnings,
we wait.

With Jesus in the desert, and in the garden,
because he asks us to,
we wait.

Echoes a prayer of The Wild Goose Resources Group

The cross, we shall take it

The cross –
we shall take it.
The Bread –
we shall break it.
The pain –
we shall bear it.
The joy –
we shall share it.
The Gospel –
we shall live it.
The Love –
we shall give it.
The Light –
we shall cherish it.
The dark –
God shall perish it.
John Bell

Jesus, Saviour of the world

Jesus, Saviour of the world,
come to us in your mercy.
We look to you to save and help us.
By your Cross and your life laid down,
you set your people free.
We look to you to save and help us.
When they were ready to perish,
you saved your disciples.
We look to you to save and help us.
In the greatness of your mercy,
free us from our chains.
Forgive the sins of all your people.
Make yourself known as our Saviour
and mighty deliverer.
Save us and help us that we may praise you.

Come now and dwell with us,
Lord Christ Jesus.
Hear our prayer and be with us always.
And when you come in your glory,
may we be one with you
and share the life of your kingdom.

My people, what wrong have I done to you?

The imagined reproaches of the Eternal Son of God to the people of the world. Suitable for Good Friday and Friday Vigils.

All sing (to the tune 'Glory be to Jesus' by Thomas Ken)

**Lord, have mercy on us, cleanse us from our sins.
Lord, have mercy on us, turn our hearts again.**

My people, what wrong have I done to you?
I am your Creator, I have entrusted the land to you,
yet you have violated its laws
and misused my creatures.
My people, what wrong have I done to you?
What good have I not done to you?
Answer me.

Lord . . .

I entrusted the world to you,
yet you have polluted its air
and created the means to destroy it.
My people, what wrong have I done to you?
What good have I not done for you?
Answer me.

Lord . . .

I made you in my likeness,
yet you have marred my image,
degraded body and soul.
I made my children of one blood
to live in families rejoicing in one another,
but you have embittered the races
and divided the peoples.
My people, what wrong have I done to you?
What good have I not done for you?
Answer me.

Lord . . .

I freed you from slavery;
yet you handed me over to death and jeered at me.
I opened the sea before you:
you opened my side with a spear!
My people, what wrong have I done to you?
What good have I not done for you?
Answer me.

Lord . . .

I fed you in the desert,
guided you with cloud by day and night,
yet you led me to Pilate!
I struck down rulers who would have harmed
you yet you struck me with a reed.
My people, what wrong have I done to you?
What good have I not done for you?
Answer me.

Lord...

I gave you from the rock living waters
of salvation;
you gave me bitter drink, you quenched my
thirst with vinegar!
What good have I not done for you?
Answer me.

Lord...

I put the sceptre into your hand
and made you a royal people;
you crowned me with the crown of thorns!
I made you great by my boundless power;
you hanged me on the gallows of the cross!
My people, what wrong have I done to you?
What good have I not done for you?
Answer me.

Lord...

I gave you my teachings,
but you have eschewed integrity,
I have come to you in this your land,
yet you have betrayed my sacrifice
and spurned my love!

Lord...

We believe, O God of all gods (Patrick's Creed)

We believe, O God of all gods,
that you are the eternal God of life.

**We believe, O God of all peoples,
that you are the eternal God of love.**

We believe that you create earth and seas
and skies,
**we believe that you create us in your image,
and give us eternal worth.**

Longer alternative version:

We believe, O God of all gods,
that you are the eternal Creator of life.

**We believe, O God of all gods,
that you are the eternal Creator of love.**

We believe, O Lord and God of all people,
that you are the Creator of the skies above,
that you are the Creator of the oceans below.

**We believe, O Lord and God of all people,
that you are the One who created our souls
and set their course,**
that you are the One
who created our bodies from earth,
that you gave to our bodies their breath
and to our souls their possession.

**God, bless to us our bodies.
God, bless to us our souls.
God, bless to us our living.
God, bless to us our goals.**

Christ Jesus – The song of Christ's glory

Christ Jesus, though you were in the form
of God
you did not cling to equality with God.
You emptied yourself,
taking the form of a servant;
you were born in human likeness.

Being found in human form you humbled yourself
and became obedient, even to death on a cross.
Therefore God has highly exalted you
and given you a name above every other name.
That at the name of Jesus every knee should bow,
in heaven and on earth and under the earth,
and every tongue confess that Jesus Christ is Lord,
to the glory of God the Father. For ever and ever.
Amen.

Philippians 2:6-11

Come, Holy Spirit, our souls inspire

Come, Holy Spirit, our souls inspire
and lighten with eternal fire.
Implant in us your grace from above,
enter our minds and hearts with love.

O come, anointing Spirit of peace,
well-spring of life and gentleness.
Past ages called you the Paraclete,
your gifts you bring to make us complete.

You are the Power of God's right hand,
promise of Christ to church and land.
Life-giving words to us impart,
renew and water our wilting heart.

Into our souls your love now pour,
refresh our weak frames with strength and power.
Give grace and courage to endure,
cast far away the evil power.

Grant us your peace throughout our days,
with you as Guide in all our ways,
no power on earth can cause us harm
and we shall know as we are known.

Teach us the Trinity to know,
the Father, Son and Spirit, too;
the Three in One and One in Three,
now and for ever, eternally.

*Adapted by Ray Simpson from Veni Creator,
ascribed to Rabanus Maurus, a sixth-century
Solitary in Gaul*

With John, the loved disciple . . . we shall overcome

With John, the loved disciple who soars like an eagle,
we shall overcome.
With the desert fathers and mothers
who were weaned from selfish living,
we shall overcome.
With Ninian of the shining Household of Faith
we shall overcome.
With Illtyd, holy and learned sage,
we shall overcome.
With David, flame and faith-builder of Wales,
we shall overcome.
With Patrick, slave of Christ and apostle of the Irish,
we shall overcome.
With Brigid, midwife of faith to the people,
we shall overcome.
With Mungo, faithful pilgrim
and founder of communities,
we shall overcome.

With Columba, Christ's giant of the Isles,
we shall overcome.
With Aidan, gentle shepherd
and apostle of England,
we shall overcome.
With Hilda, bright jewel of the Church,
gatherer of the faithful,
we shall overcome.
With Cuthbert, healer
and conqueror of the dark places,
we shall overcome.
With the saints of this place,
we shall overcome.
With . . . *(names of local or other saints may be added)*,
we shall overcome.

An alternative response for Night Prayer is
We rest in life eternal.

We shall overcome

The Lord will make us strong,
the Lord will make us strong,
the Lord will make us strong,
some day.

Chorus:
With my whole heart and mind I cry
we shall overcome some day.

Our God's Word is our shield . . .
some day.

Our hearts, they shall not yield . . .
some day.

Our Savour we'll obey . . .
today.

We'll walk the narrow way . . .
some day.
> *Echoes 'I'll overcome some day'*
> *by Charles A. Tindley*

www.ingramcontent.com/pod-product-compliance
Lightning Source LLC
Chambersburg PA
CBHW020417080526
44584CB00014B/1367